Memories
of
Luton

Part of the
Memories
series

*The Publishers would like to thank the following companies for supporting
the production of this book*

Main Sponsor
University of Luton

The Arlington Hotel

Baxter, Hart & Abraham

F & R Cawley Limited

Connolly Homes plc

W Fischer & Sons (Luton) Limited

Hayward Tyler Group

Huntleigh Healthcare

Luton Building Company Limited

Francis Little & Son Limited and AE Meeks Limited

Marida Limited

Moorlands School

Neville Funeral Service Limited

Seamarks Coach & Travel Limited

Sheaf's Dairies

SKF (UK) Limited

Thomas Brothers

The Wallis Laboratory Limited

First published in Great Britain by True North Books Limited
Units 3 - 5 Heathfield Industrial Park
Elland West Yorkshire
HX5 9AE
Tel. 01422 377977
© Copyright: True North Books Limited 1999

ISBN 1 900463 93 8

Text, design and origination by True North Books Limited
Printed and bound by The Amadeus Press Limited

Memories are made of this

Memories. We all have them; some good, some bad, but our memories of the town we grew up in are usually tucked away in a very special place in our minds. The best are usually connected with our childhood and youth, when we longed to be grown up and paid no attention to adults who told us to enjoy being young, as these were the best years of our lives. We look back now and realise that they were right.

So many memories - perhaps of the war and rationing, perhaps of parades, celebrations, Royal visits and sporting triumphs. And so many changes; one-way traffic systems and pedestrianisation. New trends in shopping that led to the very first self-service stores being opened.

Through the bad times and the good, however, Luton not only survived but prospered. We have only to look at the town as it is today, with its finest buildings restored to their full glory, and now complemented by up-to-the-minute facilities, to see what progress has been realised and what achievements have been made over the last 50 years. Luton has a history to be proud of - but more importantly, a great future to look forward to, into the new millennium and beyond.

Contents

*Events &
occasions*

Luton has long been privileged to have its royal visitors, though as we have no date for this memorable photograph we cannot say what occasion prompted this visit to the Skefko Ball Bearing Company. It could, of course, have been Skefko's Silver Jubilee, which coincided with the Silver Jubilee of King George V; alternatively, the visit could have been made the following year, when Skefko became a British public Company. The lack of a date also means, of course, that we can not be sure whether Edward was Prince of Wales or King Edward VIII at the time! His abdication could not have been too far in the future, however, as he was King for only 325 days. Edward was well-liked

for his natural charm and became known as the 'Society Prince', and many must have hoped that he would be allowed to marry the woman he loved. But Wallis Simpson had been divorced twice, the King was Head of the Church of England - and the Church's teaching on divorce was clear. Edward signed the Instrument of Abdication on the 10th December 1936, and the document was witnessed by his three brothers. His younger brother - now King George VI - gave him the title Duke of Windsor, and he left England's shores to live abroad, marrying Wallis Simpson the following June. He returned to his native country only a few times during the rest of his life.

Right: The Silver Jubilee of King George V and Queen Mary was an opportunity for Britons to state their patriotism, and every town and village made their own plans to deck windows and doorways with red, white and blue garlands, hang bunting across every street and run up the Union Jack from every flagpole. Luton put her back into the country-wide party, and held many special events to celebrate the occasion. Snapped from Market Hill, the photograph shows the carnival parade as it passed along Park Street. George Duke of York came to the throne in 1910. The model of the ideal Englishman, King George had made himself immensely popular with his subjects without really trying. He was tolerant of people whose opinions differed from his own - but not afraid to speak his mind when the occasion called for straight talking. Dignified, fair, conscientious and modest, he once remarked on the warmth with which people greeted him during his Silver Jubilee celebrations, 'I am beginning to think they like me for myself.' George V was the first monarch to broadcast a Christmas Day message over the radio; the Christmas Broadcast became the established tradition that we still enjoy today. King George died in 1936; his widow, Queen Mary, lived on until 1953.

Above: The coronation celebrations that were held on 12th May 1937 did not go according to the original plan. In the event the monarch being crowned was not Edward VIII, who had been expected to reign after the death of King George V, but his younger brother, Albert, Duke of York. The street parties, however, went ahead as planned, and in May Street people dug out their flags, streamers - and any Christmas decorations that seemed appropriate to the occasion - and used them, to the delight of the local children, to turn the street into a feast of colour.
The party in May Street was a great occasion for the little community, though the number of warm coats worn by the residents would infer that the day was cool for May. We can't be certain of that, however, as 'Ne'er cast a clout till May is out' was the adage that most people adhered to back in the 1930s.

'GR' read the initials on the banners hung in George Street to welcome King George VI to the throne; Luton was determined to be loyal to the new sovereign, even though his brother King Edward VIII had been a charming and popular man. Prince Albert had been hurled unexpectedly into the kingship he had not been trained for when Edward VIII, his older brother, who was king for a mere 325 days, renounced the throne on 10th December 1936 for American divorcee Wallis Simpson, 'the woman I love'.

The new king was shy and nervous and suffered from an embarrassing stammer (which he later overcame with medical aid and the support of his

A glance at the 1930s

HOT OFF THE PRESS
The years of the 1930s saw Adolf Hitler's sickening anti-Jewish campaign echoed in the streets of Britain. On 19th October 1936 Oswald Mosley's 7,000-strong British Union of Fascists clashed head on with thousands of Jews and Communists in London, resulting in 80 people being injured in the ensuing battle. Mosley and his 'blackshirts' later rampaged through the streets beating up Jews and smashing the windows of their businesses.

THE WORLD AT LARGE
In India, Gandhi's peaceful protests against British rule were gathering momentum. The Salt Laws were a great bone of contention: forced to buy salt from the British government, thousands of protestors marched to the salt works, intending to take it over in the name of the Indian people. Policemen and guards attacked the marchers, but not one of them fought back. Gandhi, who earned for himself the name 'Mahatma' - Great Soul - was assassinated in 1948.

ROYAL WATCH
The talking point of the early 1930s was the affair of the Prince of Wales, who later became King Edward VIII, and American divorcee Wallis Simpson. Faced with a choice, Edward gave up his throne for 'the woman I love' and spent the remainder of his life in exile. Many supported him, though they might not have been as keen to do so if they had been aware of his Nazi sympathies, kept strictly under wraps at the time.

wife Queen Elizabeth). 'I'm only a naval officer,' he confessed to his cousin Lord Louis Mountbatten on the day he became king. 'It's the only thing I know about.' He had never seen a state paper in his life. But he rose to the challenge, squared his shoulders, and adopted the title of George VI. King George VI went on to take his place as perhaps Britain's most well loved monarch.

Both pictures: Everyone loves a parade, especially if there is a band to provide foot-tapping music to keep everyone in step, and huge crowds turned out to watch the ASE-AEU Procession on 16th June 1951. The big occasion was to mark the Union's Centenary (1851-1951), and it was George Kent's brass band that led the way through the streets of Luton *(right)*. Marching behind their banners were the Union's committee men, and ingeniously decorated floats representing the town's various industries followed on behind. The event also launched 'Ludun Ltd', a non profit-making company that had been formed to employ the severely disabled, aiming to give them confidence in themselves and their abilities, and a new level of self assurance through doing a good job and being paid for their work, like the rest of society. Floats and tableaux were entered by a long list of local companies such as Percival Aircraft, Electrolux - whose float promoted their refrigerators - Skefko, Portland Cement, Commer Cars, Empire Rubber and many more. Vauxhall were of course represented *(below),* their float informing the crowd (who of course already knew) that 'Vauxhall Motors exports cover the world'. Their 1904 Vauxhall car, with its driver and passenger wearing appropriate costume, drew many admiring glances from the onlookers as it passed by. The procession made its way to Wardown sports ground, where Dr Brian Shaw explained what Ludun Ltd was all about. A great occasion that was long-remembered by those who watched or took part in the procession that day.

Above: Mention Luton and people - even today, more than 20 years after the choir disbanded - immediately think 'Girls' Choir'. But when the choir was formed back in 1936 there was no thought of the international fame that eventually became theirs. The world-famous choir sprang from Ceylon Baptist Church, where Arthur Davies conducted a small junior choir consisting of both boys and girls. He later dropped the boys to concentrate on female voices, and the new choir began to experience uncommon success. Two radio broadcasts were given by the choir in 1936, which in itself was an amazing achievement. Another incredible fact to Arthur Davies' credit, and of course that of the girls', was that very few of the choir members could read music. But Davies was a born teacher, knew exactly what he wanted his choir to achieve, and had the patience to coach the girls to musical perfection. This particular performance marked the Silver Jubilee of the Luton Girls' Choir in 1960, and the venue was Luton College of Technology.

Above right: The Queen was about to be crowned, and party time lay ahead for Luton. But before the parties came the more solemn moments. Crowds gathered around the war memorial in George Street on coronation morning to attend the open air service held in the town, and together they asked God's blessing on the country's new sovereign.
Unlike her father King George VI, the young and pretty new Queen had begun her training for the throne early, when Edward VIII's abdication in 1936 made her the

heir presumptive to the throne. She was only 14 years old when she broadcast messages of encouragement to the children of war-torn Britain, and as the war progressed she gradually took on more and more public duties. Many Lutonians saw the coronation on television, and even viewed in black and white the occasion was a memorable one. The sight of the new queen being anointed with oil and having the crown placed upon her head is one which few can forget.
The news on the morning of the coronation carried another report that the world had been waiting for - New Zealander Edmund Hillary, with John Hunt and Sherpa Tensing, had reached the summit of Everest. The Daily Express headline said it all: 'All this and Everest Too'!

Right: When the Queen was crowned in Westminster Abbey on 2nd June 1953, A mere eight years after the end of World War II, the nation relaxed for the first time and really went to town on the celebrations that welcomed her to the throne. Each town and city, every village institute and church, held their own event, which could range from a simple street party to a big parade. Along with the rest of Britain, Lutonians let their hair down. It was important to them to make sure the children had a good time on Coronation day; after all, weren't they the 'new Elizabethans'? So the ladies donned their aprons while their menfolk carried the kitchen table and dining chairs out into the street. Every family chipped in and contributed towards the loaves of bread, packets of butter (or dare we suggest margarine?), sandwich fillings, jellies, cakes of every kind - and not forgetting the gallons of tea and crates of pop that would be needed. We draw a veil over the kind of beverage that the parents would switch to once the kids were all tucked up in bed....

Below: The Queen's coronation on 2nd June 1953 gave everyone a chance to declare their loyalty - and it was party time in Luton. Garlands and banners were hung in windows, lines of bunting stretched across every street, and though the weather on the big day was inclined to be cool and rather damp, it didn't stop the children from enjoying their street parties. The sun struggled through the clouds to bless the Coronation Procession watched by thousands of enthusiastic Lutonians.

The coronation was a red letter day in the diary of everyone in town. Not only were there the official events such as the carnival parade to look forward to, but there were the many street parties, dances and fireworks parties to enjoy. Perhaps a few people among this crowd would have been able to watch the Westminster Abbey ceremony on television; it was the first time the coronation of a British monarch had ever been filmed. Many had never seen TV before - a difficult concept for us to grasp so many years on, when we are used to being surrounded by technology of all kinds. But for those who were privileged to be among those early viewers, the sight was one they will never forget.

Left: The Queen's coronation in 1953 gave everyone a chance to declare their loyalty to Her Majesty - and it was party time in Luton. Garlands and banners were hung in windows, lines of bunting stretched across every street, and though the weather on the big day was inclined to be cool and rather damp, it didn't stop the children from enjoying their street parties. It had been hoped that the big day would be fine and sunny, and when people woke up to grey skies instead of blue a number of parties were hastily rearranged and took place in factories, church halls and schoolrooms. The new venues saved the parties from the dreaded soggy sandwiches! These children were obviously having a great time, and lots of food, red, white and blue streamers, party hats and balloons added their own flavour to the event. Parents played a vital part in the proceedings, the mums donning aprons and making sandwiches and drinks in the kitchen (as mums always did in the 1950s) and the dads moving tables and chairs, blowing up balloons and organising the games.

Above: Coloured streamers arranged down the centre of the table are not enough to tell us whether this charming photograph was taken at a Christmas party, or was held to celebrate some other event. The old folk were obviously enjoying the occasion, however - and these four little cuties were drawing the kind of 'Aw - aren't they sweet?' response that is inevitable when tots dress up to entertain the older generation. The satin-clad pixie on the right demonstrates the flying power of her wings, while a second cuddles up on Gran's knee. What was the concert that they had been part of, we wonder? Were they the Fairy Godmother's little helpers in 'Cinderella' - or were they perhaps part of the fairy retinue in 'Sleeping Beauty'? Sadly, we will never know. We have no date for this lovely photograph, but the four little pixies will now have children and perhaps grandchildren of their own to entertain them in their turn.

Both pages: The Queen's main duty when she and Prince Philip visited Luton on 2nd November 1962 was to make an extended visit to the newly-opened Central Library. After being greeted by Major Simon Whitbread, Lord Lieutenant of Bedfordshire, in the pouring rain, the Queen took the royal salute from a guard of honour formed from the First Battalion the Bedfordshire and Hertfordshire Regiment, Territorial Army. As she inspected the Guard of Honour, *(this page top)* - holding her own umbrella - crowds of eager Lutonians rushed across Manchester

Square to get a better view of Her Majesty.
The royal couple were then escorted to the library, where the Borough Librarian, Frank Gardner, and the Borough Architect, Mervyn Blackman, were among those fortunate enough to be presented to the Queen. Their first duty at the library was in fact

a real treat - a short concert, staged for the royal couple by the Luton Girls' Choir. The concert set the cheerful scene for a tour of the library's up to the minute facilities. A visit to the children's story room, the Fairy Castle, was a special pleasure for the Queen, and the couple were presented with a set of books for the royal children. Prince Philip was pleased to see on the library shelves copies of his own books, 'Prince Philip speaks' and 'Birds from Britannia'.

The rain stopped falling for a while as the Queen and Prince Philip (walking behind the Mayor), to the delight of the watching crowds took a walkabout outside the library *(below left)*. Every available viewpoint was taken up by people who were determined not to miss a thing, and they positioned themselves at every nearby first floor window - and even the roof of the Co-op!

Her Majesty smiles a smile of genuine delight *(facing page, bottom)* as she unveils the plaque commemorating her visit to the new Central Library. Hundreds of children were among the crowds of people who waited in the centre of Luton to catch a glimpse of the Queen, but none could have been happier than nine year old Lynne Drummond. Few people are privileged to actually meet the Queen, but Lynne had the rare pleasure of presenting Her Majesty with the posy of flowers we see her holding. Lynne was the daughter of Luton's Mayor, Councillor Hugh Drummond (seen with the Queen in the photograph) and his wife the Mayoress. The steadily falling rain did little to dampen the enthusiasm of the crowds who waited to welcome the Queen, and the visit was a huge success. The sun shone as she left the library after her tour of Luton's brand new facility.

At leisure

Above: *Exactly what prompted this marvellous photograph we do not know, but this great crowd of mainly young people posed on the two diving boards and chute were certainly out to enjoy themselves in Luton's open air swimming pool. Judging by the style of the swim wear (many of the men are still sporting those one-piece swimming costumes), the pool could well have been very new at the time. The wonderful facility in Bath Road was opened in 1935, and on warm days during the summer months it was a very popular way to spend the day; its popularity had been foreseen, and the pool had the capacity to take around 900 swimmers. The weather had to be very warm, however, before many would brave the goose pimples, but there were always some intrepid souls who would defy the British weather to don their swimming costumes at Luton's outdoor pool. Scenes such as this one eventually became a thing of the past, and in 1989, when the fabric of the pool lining began to crack, the facility closed down. There is still hope, however, that the necessary finance will be found to renovate and re-open the pool.*

All the fun of the fair - and this fairground - date unknown - was as usual held in Wardown Park. Luton has long been seriously into enjoying its leisure time, and regular twice-yearly fairs, at Whitsuntide (Spring Bank Holiday) and summer, have long been part of the town's calendar. Add to that the circuses that still come to town and you have all the ingredients for real enjoyment.

Luton fair always had an atmosphere of its very own that had to be experienced to be appreciated. The whirr and hum of the rides, the loud beat of the music, several different tunes fighting with each other for attention, the shouts of the man who bravely volunteered to guess your weight, the squeals of the girls as they spun around on the waltzer. And the food! The shocking pink candy floss that was sold from booths and was spun around a stick while you waited, the toffee apples, dark red and shining as if they had been varnished, the paper bags of crunchy brandy snap and the ice cream, in tubs, cornets or wafers. All very thrilling stuff, and calculated to send any child home tired and satisfied at the end of a wonderful day out.

This page: Between 1936 and 1976 the Luton Girls' Choir sang in front of every member of the British royal family, even finding themselves in demand for a Royal Command Performance *(right)*. Though a number of them were obviously much younger, the average age of choir members was 18. The singers had quite a short 'shelf life' however, as in order to adhere to their description as a 'girls" choir, its members were retired either when they reached the age of 23 or got married, whichever happened first. Though over the years the choir brought in many thousands of pounds for charity, the girls themselves gave their services free, enjoying making music for its' own sake. In actual fact, a small charge was made for the privilege of belonging to the Luton Girls' Choir! A wide range of charities benefited from the choir's performances, from a church being provided with a new organ to donations made to the National Children's Homes.

During their first three years the choir gave more than 200 concerts, and by the end of the 1950s the fame of the Luton Girls' Choir was spreading quickly. In 1959 they embarked on a three-month tour of Australia and New Zealand, and they are seen here boarding their plane ready for the big adventure *(top)*. Plane spotters will recognise that the aircraft is a KLM Royal Dutch Airlines Lockheed Constellation. The tour was a runaway success, and the girls travelled an amazing 35,000 miles and gave a total of 93 concerts. The choir was disbanded in 1976, shortly before the death of Arthur Davies; this was at his own request. In 1986 however, the Luton Girls' Choir held a reunion to celebrate the 50th anniversary of the formation of the choir; the 60th anniversary was marked by a further reunion of 200 former choir members, sadly the last.

This page: How many of our readers can admit to having been one of St Mary's angelic choirboys in the days before approaching manhood sent their voices plunging from treble to baritone? The impressive size of St Mary's church choir reflects the standing of one of the largest parish churches in England, and in this group photograph, thought to date from the 1950s, *(bottom)* the male members far outnumber the female - a fact that is worth remarking on, as it is thought that more women then men regularly attend church. Being part of St Mary's choir was obviously something that musical Lutonians could be proud of, and the choirboys in the earlier photograph taken in 1938 *(below left)* grin cheerfully for the camera as they process from St Mary's Hall to the church.

St Mary's was built at different times in ancient days - the oldest church to be built on the site was back in 931. The building we know today was consecrated in 1137, though at that time it was considerably smaller; it was added to over the years to meet the increase in the local population, giving us the magnificent church that still impresses visitors with its beauty. Its remarkable stone and flint chequer work was originally confined to the church tower before being extended to the rest of the church building. In 1968 further additions were made, providing parishioners with a hall, vestry and church offices, though every care was taken to ensure that the new facilities merged tastefully with the old architecture.

Bottom: The Hatters in early days - this was the squad back in the late 1930s, when the clouds of war hung low over Britain. The declaration of war on 3rd September 1939 brought an immediate blanket ban on sport, and many sportsmen and women immediately enlisted in the services. It was Winston Churchill's £50,000 campaign urging the nation to cheerfulness that was later to give soccer a new lease of life.

Luton Town Football Club had been formed back in 1885, with Excelsior's as their ground; they moved to Kenilworth Road in 1905. The first years at the new ground were not good ones for the club and the 1911-12 season saw relegation to Southern League Division Three. After the first world war, however, the situation began to improve; in 1920 the club rejoined the Football League and played in Division Three. By the 1930s things began to buzz, backed by the appointment of players like Joe Payne and Freddie Roberts. Further glory lay ahead for the Hatters; 1955 brought them promotion to the First Division.

Right: 'We want Joe! We want Joe!' Joe Payne's adoring fans went wild with joy back in May 1937, storming the pitch at Kenilworth Road after the match that clinched the Town's promotion to the Second Division. Already famed as a peerless striker (only the year before he had scored an amazing 10 goals in one match against Bristol Rovers!), Payne had scored both goals in the key match that gave the Hatters a 2-0 win over Torquay United, and he was the hero of the day. Fans crowded in front of the main stand shouting for their champion until he came out along with Nelson to make a speech.

The appointment of Ned Liddell as manager had paid off; at the start of the season he had expressed his confidence in the team and in their ability to win promotion - and events had proved him right. With Payne leading the way, Luton Town's total of 103 goals in 42 games had brought them the coveted promotion, and now it was time for the champagne to flow.

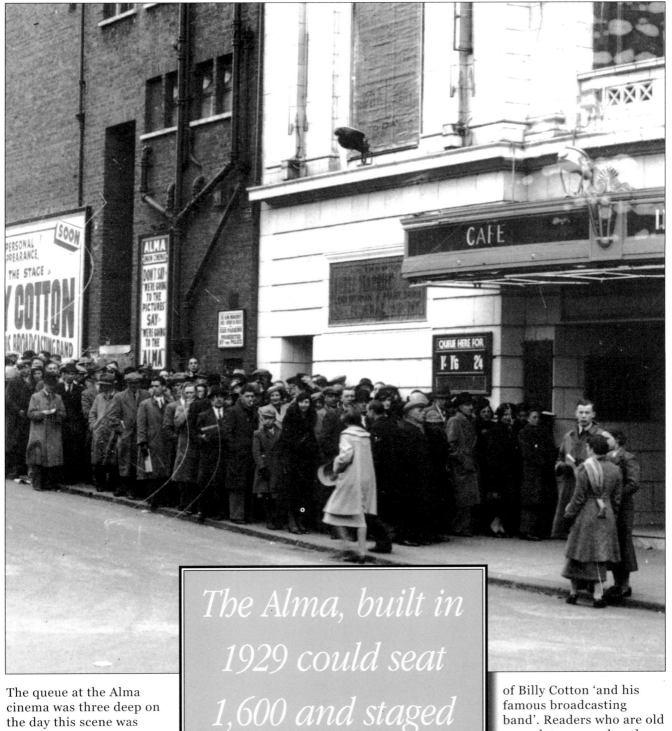

The Alma, built in 1929 could seat 1,600 and staged live shows as well as films

The queue at the Alma cinema was three deep on the day this scene was captured; it would be fascinating to be able to read the sign by the door and find out what exactly what was showing at the time! The grand sum of one shilling (five new pence) would secure you a reasonably good seat, but if you wanted real luxury you could always dig deep for that special 2/4d seat - around 12 pence in today's currency, if not in value. The Alma staged live shows as well as films, and coming soon, a large notice tells us, was a 'personal appearance on stage'

of Billy Cotton 'and his famous broadcasting band'. Readers who are old enough to remember the 1950s will be instantly reminded of his loud cry of 'Wakey Wakey!' that introduced 'The Billy Cotton Band Show'. Sunday lunchtime, wasn't it? Whenever the radio show went out, the citizens of Luton were due for a memorable time when the great bandleader visited the town in person. The Alma, built in 1929, had a seating capacity of more than 1,600; it was demolished in 1960 for redevelopment.

Wartime

Both pages: These evacuees, each one labelled like a parcel, looked so forlorn that they tugged at the heartstrings of the people of Luton *(left)*. It looks as though a drink of cold water was all that was on offer at this particular moment, but as the long crocodiles of children made their way from the railway station to their dispersal centre at Dunstable Road Junior school, people came out of their houses to offer the little visitors drinks of tea or milk. It was 1st September 1939, and though war had not yet been officially declared, the safety of children who lived in high-risk areas was a priority. Evacuation was a wise move, but it surely took great courage on the part of the parents of these children, to see them packed them off to other parts of the country where they would be put into the care of strangers. Many of the kiddies had already said goodbye to fathers (some of them for the last time) who had already signed up for military service.

Not all of those who arrived in Luton ended up staying in the town. Many of them were sent on by coach to surrounding areas *(below)*. The first 537 children to arrive in the town with their teachers came from schools in Walthamstow; some of them were billeted with families in Luton while others went on to Dunstable and Barton. But trains continued to arrive throughout the day, bringing almost 5,000 children and their teachers into the town. Not everything went to plan on the second day, however, when the timetable of arrivals by rail was altered. Parties began to arrive by road, including groups of blind people with their carers; many mothers with small children descended on the town having made their own travel arrangements - and householders who had been expecting children to be billeted with them were not quite as keen to receive adults into their homes. Organisation became a nightmare for staff at the dispersal centre; during the three days of 'Operation Pied Piper' more than 12,000 evacuees were processed through Dunstable Road School. Eight thousand of them remained in the town, and the people of Luton were praised for the way they opened their homes to the young strangers. Within a few weeks, however, around half of the Londoners had returned home, unable to adapt to the new surroundings and the different way of life.

They had no idea where they would be sleeping that night, but these children evacuated from London look cheerful all the same. To most of them, this was a big adventure, and clutching their gas masks, cases, packets of food and teddy bears, they descended on Luton in their thousands. In 1938 Adolf Hitler had signed the Munich Agreement and Britain's Prime Minister, Neville Chamberlain, made the mistake of trusting him. Many, however, had no confidence in Hitler and couldn't believe Chamberlain's assurance of 'peace in our time'; they continued to prepare for a war that they still saw as inevitable. London would be

A glance at the 1940s

WHAT'S ON?
In wartime Britain few families were without a wireless set. It was the most popular form of entertainment, and programmes such as ITMA and Music While You Work provided the people with an escape from the harsh realities of bombing raids and ration books. In 1946 the BBC introduced the Light Programme, the Home Service and the Third Programme, which gave audiences a wider choice of listening.

GETTING AROUND
October 1948 saw the production of Britain's first new car designs since before the war. The Morris Minor was destined for fame as one of the most popular family cars, while the four-wheel-drive Land Rover answered the need for a British-made off-road vehicle. The country was deeply in the red, however, because of overseas debts incurred during the war. The post-war export drive that followed meant that British drivers had a long wait for their own new car.

SPORTING CHANCE
American World Heavyweight Boxing Champion Joe Louis, who first took the title back in 1937, ruled the world of boxing during the 1940s, making a name for himself as unbeatable. Time after time he successfully defended his title against all comers, finally retiring in 1948 after fighting an amazing 25 title bouts throughout his boxing career. Louis died in 1981 at the age of 67.

Hitler's obvious target in the expected bombing raids, so it was vital that children were evacuated to safe areas.
Long before war was declared, billeting officers had been appointed by the government to look for suitable accommodation for children and expectant mothers in towns that were seen as secure areas. Luton was lined up to take a total of 22,000 from Walthamstow and London.

Bottom: It's 'Eyes right!' as a unit of the Bedfordshire and Hertfordshire Home Guard Regiment march past the saluting base in front of the Town Hall back in 1940.

During the second world war military parades had become an accepted part of life, and were a real morale-booster; children loved the excitement of the rousing bands and the marching soldiers, and the parades undoubtedly made the average person in the street feel in touch with the military and the progress of the war.

Many members of the Home Guard had never before so much as wielded a broom handle in anger, but they were all prepared to do their bit for Britain.

At the beginning of World War II, men outside military age were asked to join a force of amateur soldiers in defence of their country in the event of invasion by Germany. They trained hard to meet the standards required of them.

The force, even if amateur, was very well organised. If parachutes were seen landing, the local church bells would be rung to summon the unpaid volunteers from their normal jobs of work. Compensation would be made for any loss of wages caused by a call to action stations.

Right: During the second world war, aeroplane manufacture was very close to the hearts of Lutonians, and hundreds of them congregated in the streets during Wings for Victory Week. Here, the Percival Aircraft factory workers - every one in step - march past Col Milton S Turner, Acting Air Attaché, who took the salute. Percival Aircraft Ltd, who were established in Luton in 1936, were in 1944 taken over by the Hunting Group. In 1960, Hunting Aircraft Ltd became part of the British Aircraft Corporation.

The British public were bombarded with appeals for help during World War II; War Weapons Week was staged in 1940, Warships in 1942, Wings for Victory in 1943 and Save the Soldier in 1944. Thousands of pounds were raised for the war effort, but more importantly people felt that they were doing their part, however small, in winning the war. Fund raising served as a great morale-booster.

> *The first sign of attack came from a single plane circling the town*

Old Bedford Road bore the brunt of Nazi fury during a daring daylight bombing raid on October 15th 1940. It was just before noon when the sirens sounded. Eyewitnesses spotted a single plane circling Luton - and saw it drop a large bomb. For the hat factories of Old Bedford Road the attack could hardly have come at a worse time, as everyone was at work - mostly women and girls. W O Scales & Co were worst hit; 13 of their employees were killed and 35 injured - the youngest of them being a boy of 14

who was badly hurt and had to be given morphia during the rescue. The blast blew the factory apart, scattering heavy sewing machines and a blocking machine around the nearby roofs and gardens like leaves, while ribbons and pieces of material hung grotesquely from the trees like alien fruit. Not too far away, safe in their air raid shelter below the playground at Old Bedford Road School, sat hundreds of children who thankfully survived what was in fact one of Luton's worst wartime bombing raids.

This page: Pretty girls often helped to promote an appeal, and during the World War II Wings for Victory Week, Miss Luton (Dilys Evans) worked hard at fund raising. Her activities that week included making a tour of local factories. One of her stop-offs was at Davis Gas Stoves, where Miss Luton was pictured with some of the workers *(above)*. The company's presence in Luton dated back to the late 19th century, and they became known for the Diamond gas cooker, which appeared on the market during the same year as Queen Victoria's Jubilee was celebrated.

At the Electrolux factory in Oakley Road Miss Luton's fund raising efforts were backed up by Miss Electrolux, Mary Taylor *(right);* was this auto truck their means of transport around the works, we wonder? It could have been fun, though the beauty queens' dress was hardly suitable.... Electrolux were a large employer in Luton, producing vacuum cleaners and refrigerators. They were set to become one of the largest and most up to date factories producing refrigerators in Europe;

Electrolux were the first British manufacturer to hit the two million output in domestic fridges; the factory closed in October 1998.

Wings for Victory Week involved every club, school, pub and organisation who could organise events and raise a few pounds, and indicators were erected everywhere with pointers that rose slowly towards the agreed target.

This page: It's Warship Week in Luton (7th - 14th March 1942), and collecting boxes are being rattled beneath the noses of shoppers in George Street by local Civil Defence workers and the British Legion *(below)*. The plangent tones of a pianola being played from the back of a horse and cart jolly up the event as people are invited to dig deep into their pockets and contribute to the worthy cause. The horse-drawn vehicle - and possibly the pianola itself - has very likely been loaned by George Kent Ltd, bringing to mind the days when noise from the town's traffic involved only the rattle of wheels and the trotting of hooves, and the only traffic pollution could be put to good use on the land. Petrol was strictly rationed during World War II, and the

trusty four-legged mode of transport was in evidence everywhere during the 1940s and even into the 50s. Thousands of Lutonians contributed to the morale-boosting Warship Week, and at the end of the appeal, crowds of people congregated in front of the target indicator near the Town Hall. Warship Week coincided with a royal visit from King Peter of Yugoslavia - perhaps the King was present at the time of this photograph *(bottom)*.

The public were asked at regular intervals to contribute to one worthy cause or another during the war, whether it was in giving their odd sixpences and shillings, donating their alminium saucepans and tin baths (supposedly to help build battleships and aeroplanes,

though little of the scrap collected ever left the scrapyards), or giving clothes, books and food to organisations such as the Red Cross and the RVS. The war effort prompted much rivalry between local firms; the larger ones might raise £20,000 for a Wellington Bomber (to be repaid after the war), while small companies might manage to get a couple of thousand pounds together to pay for an aeroplane wing. Collections in public houses were more modest, aspiring to £30 for a sub-machine gun or £138 for a 2,000lb bomb. A donation from an individual with a few coppers to spare might be 6d for a rivet or perhaps four shillings for a hand grenade.

Many towns and cities actually 'bought' Spitfires for £5,000; a list of contributors to the war effort was read out over the wireless every day after the evening news.

Left: There was more to look at in Luton than shop windows on 12th August 1941, and this Valentine tank making a show visit to the town soon attracted a small crowd of admirers to its position at the foot of Market Hill. World War II was in full swing, and the visible presence of tanks, weapons and military parades around the streets of Britain had proved to be great morale-boosters. Little boys in particular were drawn to the demonstration like flies to a honeypot, probably bombarding the attendant ATS corporal and sergeant who were staffing the tank with a never-ending list of questions. These boys would be comparing the Valentine with the Churchill tank, which they knew all about; the Churchill was made locally by many of their dads (and mums too) at the Vauxhall works. During World War II, Vauxhall slowed their production of private cars to concentrate on building vehicles for the services. The spectacular 38-ton Churchill tank was designed and built by Vauxhall within twelve months - an incredible feat, as it would normally take around four years to produce such a vehicle.

Above: During World War II the dazzling white stone of the Town Hall was toned down by the use of sacking as camouflage; not attractive to look at, certainly, but it made sure that the Town Hall was considerably less attractive as a target for enemy bombs. It was Warship Week 1942 when this photograph was taken, and the huge indicator for the target sum can be seen in the distance near the war memorial. How many older Lutonians remember visiting the Ark Royal Exhibition? We know that the date of the photograph is correct, though the reason for the 'GR' banners hung around George Street is less obvious. George VI was crowned five years earlier on 12th May 1937, and the presence of the banners is unlikely to be an extreme case of procrastination - leaving us with a little mystery!

George Street has changed almost beyond recognition today, as later years gave us the Arndale to the right of the photograph, and a pleasant pedestrianised area with street entertainment, pavement cafes and street traders. Today, undercover shopping centres have become a popular and accepted part of modern life, and people can now 'shop till they drop' in the comfort of a controlled environment. Being able to browse around their favourite stores that are under one roof and are therefore sheltered from cold winds and driving rain holds great appeal for shoppers running the gauntlet of the British climate.

Success in the highest degree

As the new millennium commences education is rarely out of the national news, with the Government regularly revising the examination framework modifying new methods of assessment and new performance indicators for teachers and pupils alike. The ultimate aim of all this change, of course, is to raise educational standards. None locally since the late nineteenth century has featured more prominently as Luton has sought its own answer to the question of how best to improve the standard of education. Progress towards this was finally delivered on 14th July 1993 when Luton College of Higher Education was granted authority by the Privy Council to change its name to the University of Luton.

A hundred years ago Luton was a very long way from being a university town. Up until the last decade of the 19th century, the town's principal industry had been the manufacture of straw hats, a trade where a formal education was widely considered to be of no very great value. However, there were those, such as hat manufacturer Charles Warren and F W Beck, a local solicitor

and a member of the Chamber of Commerce, who felt strongly that Luton should be offering some form of technical and commercial education. Unfortunately, support from Bedfordshire County Council was not forthcoming, partly because Luton's needs as a town were developing in a very different direction to the more rural interests of the rest of the county.

The need for vocational training in Luton became more acute when new industries began to find their way to the town in the 1890s, with encouragement from the New Industries Committee set up by the Borough and the Chamber of Commerce. The approval of companies such as Vauxhall and SKF brought tremendous new employment opportunities - for those with the skills to take advantage of them. Finally, following the Education Act of 1902, Luton was able to take its first, and arguably overdue, step towards the establishment

Below: *Park Square, looking towards what was to become the site of the Technical College. The picture dates from 1902.*

College, and in 1988 the Modern School and Technical College formally separated when this formed and moved to a purpose built site elsewhere in the town.

The first section of the building programme was effected in 1936. Construction work then proceeded as best it could throughout the second world war with wooden huts providing temporary accommodation when necessary; the second phase was begun in 1940 and completed the following year, and by 1948 the third phase, too, was substantially completed. However, at that point the situation was reviewed. There had been an increasing recognition of the importance of the role of technical vocation education in ensuring the continued expansion of industry in the town and the surrounding South Bedfordshire area, and the Authority met with the Ministry of Education to discuss what future provision ought to be made. As a result of this meeting a revised schedule of

of an institute of professional education with the construction of its 'Secondary School', or 'Modern School' as it was later known, subsequently destined to become the 'Technical College'. By the 1930s, when the population of Luton stood at around 70,000, this building was struggling to meet the town's needs; an ambitious programme of alterations and extensions was planned, to be carried out in six phases. It was decided to develop a 'Junior Technical College' within the institution which in May 1937 was renamed Luton Technical

Above: *The White House, which was built for the Burr family and became the home of the Technical College.*
Top: *Another view of Park Square, dating from 1910.*

accommodation was approved for engineering, science, building, commerce and art, with modern laboratories and workshops to be included to meet the new and additional demands.

The new schedule was more far-reaching than the previous plans, and called for a radical approach. There were many considerations to be taken into account; the new accommodation would require an extensive site, would need to be easily accessible, and ideally would make use of the buildings that had already been erected as part of the programme of alterations and extensions. Architects Norman & Dawburn, of London, were appointed to prepare a preliminary report, with sketches and a model. After much discussion it was decided that the new college should be located in the centre of the town where it would be served by all local transport services. In order to acquire a site of sufficient size, considerable redevelopment of existing properties was inevitable, and there was therefore a great deal of legal negotiation to be done with the existing tenants and occupiers. Among the buildings earmarked for demolition were a public house, a hat factory, a motor engineering works, several shops and a church, as well as the obsolescent Secondary School

Below: *Luton Modern School in 1908.*

buildings. Fortunately the representatives of local industry and commerce were prepared to co-operate fully, and all the necessary permission was obtained and arrangements made to the satisfaction of all concerned. A number of Compulsory Purchase Orders were issued, and the Trustees of the church agreed to the offer of a new building on another site, while the licence of the public house was transferred to new premises - much to the regret of many of the teaching staff, who had found its former location very convenient. A site of some two-and-a-half acres was thus made available for development. It was decided that the recently-erected building should be retained for as long as possible, for use while building work was in progress, although eventually they would have to be demolished to allow the final phase to proceed, as it proved impractical to incorporate them into the overall design of the new College.

The new accommodation was desperately needed. Classes were being held in corridors, in storerooms, in fact in any available space that the College could lay its hands on, and still in 1953 there was a waiting list of over 100 hopeful students for a workshop engineering course, but nowhere to run it. However, on May 5th 1955 the site for the first phase of construction work had been cleared and the first stone of the edifice that was to

Above: *The staff of Luton Modern School, 1908.*

become the South Bedfordshire College of Further Education was laid by Alderman John Burgoyne, a man who is remembered by Lutonians for his services to education in the town in his various capacities, as a Liberal councillor, as Chairman of the Bedfordshire County Council Education Committee, as Chairman of the Governing Body of the Technical Institute and as Mayor of Luton between 1938 and 1944. A popular local figure with a good sense of humour, he worked tirelessly to secure improved educational facilities for Luton and clearly enjoyed laying the first stone of the new building, as the following Easter he enrolled at the College for Advanced Brickwork!

The first two phases of the new building came into use from Easter 1957, and from then on the College - renamed Luton College of Technology in 1958 - was able expand in directions that would have been impossible without the new accommodation. Against a background where the 'baby boom' was approaching school leaving age, and with 50 percent of school leavers at the end of the 50s receiving no further education, expansion was clearly a priority. The first new department to be added was Electrical Engineering, and by 1960 there were eight departments in all: Mechanical and Production Engineering, Electrical Engineering, Science, Mathematics, Building, Domestic Subjects, the School of Art, and Commerce, Management and Liberal Studies.

The staff of the College had risen to 134; this figure included both administrative and academic staff but did not include visiting lecturers, of whom there were many. Close links were being forged with industry, with

representatives of local employers, industrial and commercial bodies and trades unions sitting alongside college governors on various advisory committees. This meant that the College was well placed to implement Government recommendations issued in 1956 for the development of 'sandwich' courses, and the provision of vocational training in Luton was perhaps the best anywhere in the country.

It is interesting to note that throughout the changing economic and industrial climate, hatmaking remained a popular skill and Luton College of Technology's millinery classes were held in high esteem; in 1960 one of the young ladies on the millinery course was selected by the BBC Schools Programme to be interviewed as part of a careers broadcast. Overall, however, the most popular courses at Luton College of Technology around this time were chemistry, botany and zoology, then physics and mathematics, showing a clear shift of emphasis from engineering to science subjects. Part-time students could work towards the Higher National Certificate, and those who achieved good results could then go on to study as external students for the University of London's BSc degree, as could those who achieved two passes in science and maths subjects at A-level. The college's students obtained very creditable

degree successes and soon the College was able to develop its degree provision, first by offering the BSc courses on a full-time basis, and later offering two more University of London external degrees, the BSc (Econ) and BA (General) on a part-time basis.

However, increasingly complex legislation governing further education, in combination with Luton's geographical location and its unfortunate situation right on the administrative boundaries, began to work to Luton's disadvantage during the mid-60s. The Robbins Report, in 1964, made provision for 34 colleges in England and Wales to become polytechnics, but to Luton's disappointment it was not amongst those chosen. Thereafter it found itself at a disadvantage when seeking approval to run degree-level courses, again because of its location, because of its position on the Local Education Authority boundaries and now also because it did not hold polytechnic status. Meanwhile further fundamental changes to the degree-awarding process were being introduced; the Council for National Academic Awards was set up as the body to which colleges were required to apply for validation to award degrees, and the University of London announced its intention of discontinuing the registration of full-time external students for its degrees at other institutions.

points below the qualifying threshold. However, provision was made under the act for colleges who subsequently reached this threshold to be transferred to the new Polytechnics and Colleges Funding Council sector at a later stage. An expansion of Luton College's higher education activities and increased recruitment of students onto professional courses meant that the proportion of students on higher education courses the following session did in fact exceed the stipulated threshold. The College therefore submitted an application to the Secretary of State, and in due course Luton College was admitted to the new independent sector, in spite of a considerable amount of opposition from Bedfordshire County Council. The management of the College had to present a very strong and well-supported case indeed, and it is a testimony to the commitment and strength of those concerned that Luton College was able to take its rightful place in 1989 in the first tier of public sector higher education.

There followed a period of tremendous growth for the College. A wider range of undergraduate and taught postgraduate courses was introduced, with new academic provision for degree courses in business and law, a revised and broader combined science scheme and the addition of humanities, health and social care, and media and communications studies. More opportunities for postgraduate research was created, attracting such high numbers of student enrolments that Luton College became one of the fastest-expanding institutions in the higher education sector. This achievement was the result of a well-planned strategy and a prolonged and concerted effort by the College's management and staff. As an independent institution, Luton College had to compete for students and for funding with other establishments of higher education. Bids for funding from Government sources were assessed according to an institution's price, ability to recruit, and quality, while funds were also available

Left: Girls exercising in the courtyard of Luton Modern School. Below: The 1953 class on Window Dressing which was attended by more than 80 pupils.

The College therefore embarked on the mammoth task of preparing the exhaustive documentation which would form the basis of its submission to the Council for the National Academic Awards; and it is a tribute to the determination and hard work of those involved that their submission was approved, and from 1973 on the College was able to teach its own syllabus.

The next administrative hurdle was faced by the College in 1987, when another radical change came about. Polytechnics, together with colleges of higher education where the ratio of higher education to further education provision was rated as at least 55 percent, were freed from local authority control and established as independent higher education corporations, governed by the Polytechnics and Colleges Funding Council. Again, the system worked against Luton College of Higher Education, where the higher education to further education ratio was assessed as falling several

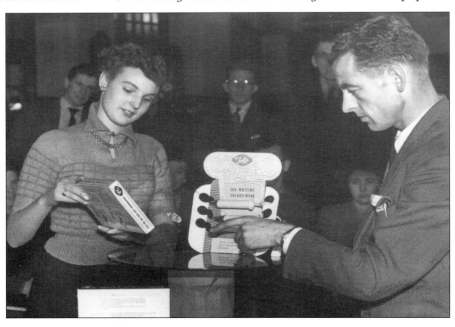

from other public agencies and through sponsorship from the private sector for those institutions who could demonstrate their suitability in terms of the courses they offered and the resources and facilities which they could provide. Luton College proved adept at securing funding from a variety of sources, and this, combined with its energetic development of new course provision and its imaginative and highly successful recruitment drives, was an important factor in its continued expansion. Meanwhile changes in the management structure of the College had been implemented which would ensure that administrative costs were kept to a minimum without adverse effect on efficiency, and a careful planned staff recruitment and development scheme had been introduced. This latter was particularly important in view of the major shift in the academic focus of the institution, with a wider range of disciplines being taught to a larger number of students at a higher level. One aspect of this was the innovatory Quality Network project, the first of its kind in higher education, which stressed to colleagues the importance of honesty, trust, respect, empowerment, consultation and teamwork; these are beliefs and values which have remained close to the heart of the institution ever since.

Another inevitable consequence of increased student numbers and a wider range of courses was, of course, that the existing accommodation and resources once again came under pressure. Greater financial independence meant that the College was now its own master in this respect, and it was able to finance the construction of a new 1,000 square metre Learning Resources Centre entirely from its own revenue. Refurbishment carried out with the help of some outside funding resulted in the provision of large, modern lecture theatres; both

these projects, along with many more, such as the conversion of an underground car park into a student social centre and the redesign of the Park Square Campus, were completed by September 1992. More residential accommodation was provided for students, with the target of being able to offer a place in purpose-built accommodation to every first-year full-time student from outside the locality. Significant additions to library resources were also made possible by income derived from company sponsorship.

Official recognition of the College's growing importance came in the form of the Council for the National Academic Awards accreditation, closely followed by the College being granted, by the Privy Council, the power to award first its own taught degrees, then in April 1993 its own research degrees as well. This was very significant for the College, as not only was it proof that the Higher Education Quality Council had been duly impressed by the quality of its teaching and its facilities, but it also meant that the College now met all the criteria required to change its name to that of University. A request was submitted to the Privy Council, and on 15th July 1993, following official confirmation that the institution could henceforth be known as the the University of Luton, celebrations began at the Great Putteridge Bury Garden Party and continued the following evening at the Grand Formal Ball. It certainly was an event to celebrate!

The University of Luton comprises four Faculties - The Luton Business School, Healthcare and Social Studies,

Below: *Rag Week 1964 style, in aid of the Freedom from Hunger campaign.*

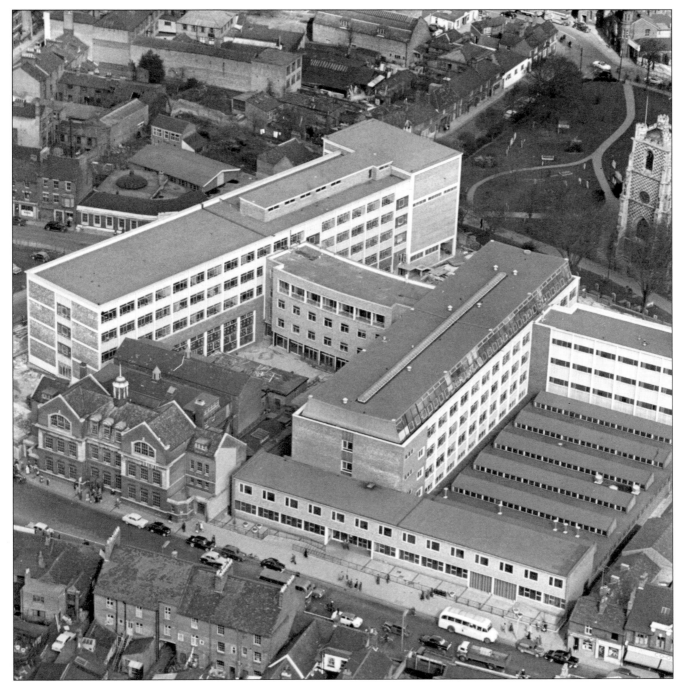

Science, Technology & Design, and Humanities, plus two Professional Centres - External Affairs and Educational Development. The student population in the academic year 1997/1998 was 10,509 (full-time equivalent) as compared with 3,200 seven years earlier; during the same five year period the academic staff had risen from 259 to 517, and the total number of staff from 529 to 1115.

Extracts from 'A Hatful of Talent' with kind permission of Dr S Bunker and Dr A Wood.

Above: *A bird's eye view of the premises in the early 1960s.* **Right:** *The new Learning Resources Centre which opened in 1992.*

Schooldays

Catch the ball as it rolled through the tunnel formed by the legs of your team mates, run to the front, roll it through again...which team will be the winner? *(below)* The photograph captures all the excitement of the school sports day - and this particular sports day was held by Moorlands School. The traditional venue was Wardown Park, and the children would have been training for many weeks in advance. Some of the races, such as this one, and others that involved dressing up, *(right)* would be fun events involving forfeits and obstacles.

Then there would be the serious events that really sorted the sheep from the goats. The hundred yards dash, the relay race, the high jump, the long jump - all would have been there, and all helping to keep the children fit and healthy. The photographs include boys as well as girls, though when Moorlands School was founded in the last decade of the 19th century, only girls were on the register. That first school building is believed to have been situated in New Bedford Road. Moorlands school became fully co-educational in the 1950s.

No fluorescent jacket was needed by Dunstable Road Junior School's first lollipop man back in 1938 - and he was unlikely to attract the distressing level of insult and abuse that today's crossing attendants often have to put up with from motorists who put children's lives in danger to save themselves a couple of minutes. Though traffic was sufficient back in the 1930s to demand the services of a crossing attendant, Dunstable Road was destined to become far busier as traffic levels built up, especially during the 60s and 70s. All the same, traffic

Between the two world wars 120,000 people were killed in traffic accidents

accidents were a real problem in the 1930s; in fact between the two world wars a staggering 120,000 people were killed in traffic accidents. Between the end of World War I and 1930 the number of cars on Britain's roads increased from around 200,000 to more than a million; the Minister of Transport, Leslie Hore Belisha, was concerned and called for new regulations. He introduced the first pedestrian crossings, and in 1934 the Road Traffic Act brought in the speed limit of 30mph in built up areas and made driving tests compulsory for new drivers.

Around the town centre

The old Carnegie Library takes up much of the background of this view, shot in May 1961, and whether you wanted to unwind with one of Miss Read's Village books, or maybe preferred something a little more humorous, such as Monica Dickens or P G Wodehouse, or enjoyed the edge-of-the-seat excitement of Agatha Christie or Edgar Wallace, there was something in the library to suit your taste in fiction. A huge selection of non-fiction would give you information about wide-ranging topics. The facility was well used by Lutonians for more than 50 years; it was demolished in 1963. The new Central Library had opened in the previous year, adding an exciting modern development to Luton's rich culture. A Boots' the Chemist store replaced it until it was itself replaced by the Arndale Centre.

Luton town centre during World War II reflected the fact that as petrol was strictly rationed more people than ever were using public transport. Fuel was expensive, too - in fact in 1940 petrol rose to 1/11d a gallon. In wartime Britain, well-intentioned notices were posted everywhere to boost the morale of the person in the street; the huge sign mounted on the Corn Exchange reminds passers by that Luton had a savings target of £33,333, which they hoped to achieve by the 30th September that year.

By the end of the 1940s the Corn Exchange had become structurally unsound, and it was demolished

in 1951. The facility was sadly missed as a venue for events of every kind whether it was a retirement party, a film show or a dance.

The windows of Boots chemists shop were in the 1940s rather dull compared with those of today, that sparkle with jewellery, hair ornaments and cosmetics. This was the place to go, however, not only to have your doctor's medicines dispensed but to buy the popular home remedies that had stood the test of time: castor oil, ipecacuanha, camphorated oil, Indian Brandee and Fennings fever powders.

A glance at the 1940s

HOT OFF THE PRESS

At the end of World War II in 1945 the Allies had their first sight of the unspeakable horrors of the Nazi extermination camps they had only heard of until then. In January, 4,000 emaciated prisoners more dead than alive were liberated by the Russians from Auschwitz in Poland, where three million people, most of them Jews, were murdered. The following year 23 prominent Nazis faced justice at Nuremberg; 12 of them were sentenced to death for crimes against humanity.

THE WORLD AT LARGE

The desert area of Alamogordo in New Mexico was the scene of the first atomic bomb detonation on July 16, 1945. With an explosive power equal to more than 15,000 tons of TNT, the flash could be seen 180 miles away.
President Truman judged that the bomb could secure victory over Japan with far less loss of US lives than a conventional invasion, and on 6th August the first of the new weapons was dropped on Hiroshima. Around 80,000 people died.

ROYAL WATCH

By the end of World War II, the 19-year-old Princess Elizabeth and her distant cousin Lieutenant Philip Mountbatten RN were already in love. The King and Queen approved of Elizabeth's choice of husband, though they realised that she was rather young and had not mixed with many other young men. The couple's wedding on 20th November 1947 was a glittering occasion - the first royal pageantry since before the war.

An unfamiliar sight to us today - George Street with traffic and without the Arndale Centre! All these buildings on the right were nearing the end of their lives and a decade or so later were replaced by modern buildings. Today Littlewoods department stores occupies

much of the space that in earlier years was taken up by smaller shops and the George Hotel. Pedestrianisation brought an end to the days when you took your life in your hands to cross George Street, and today this has to be the most elegant road in Luton. Shady booths, low walls and flower beds form a restful background for strolling shoppers, and benches where weary passers-by can sit in the sun and rest their feet, are some of the main features of George Street today.

Above: Do you remember your old Co-op 'divi' number? Hundreds of people still do! Many Co-op buildings that are considerably older than this one still stand; others have been demolished. Back in the 19th and early 20th century, many Co-operative stores were built around the towns and cities of Britain, offering local people reasonably-priced clothing and shoes as well as basic groceries. As the 20th century progressed and trends in shopping changed, many of the old Victorian premises were replaced with modern single-storey supermarket-style buildings selling mainly food products.

The Bury Park branch of the Co-op (which we are reliably informed was Number Three Branch) enjoyed a 'spearhead' position at the corner of Dunstable Road and Leagrave Road. The shopping public in Luton have been shopping at the Co-op for more than a hundred years; the very first branch opened in Luton back in 1897. During the earlier years of the 20th Century the Co-op movement was responsible for a vast improvement in the standard of living of the average British working class person.

Below: A feast of shopping memories is provoked by this view of George Street, and Trueform, Paige ladies' fashions, Meakers, Freeman, Hardy & Willis shoe shop and Marks and Spencer take us right back to the 1950s. Marks & Spencer has suffered from an unfortunate 'fuddy-duddy' image in recent years, but the quality of its clothing and the excellence of its food department has never been in doubt, and M & S remains the favourite store with thousands of shoppers. Further along on the left past Button Bros lies the Savoy Cinema, which started life in Luton in the same week as did the Odeon. The very first film to be shown there was 'Test Pilot', pilloried by at least one reviewer, who was unused to today's deafening sound-tracks, as a 'noisy' film. Produced in black and white, the film told the story of a talented pilot, his wife, and his self-sacrificing friend. The Savoy survived the threat of the bulldozer and is still showing films today under the ABC banner.

Below: How many readers remember quaffing their very first pint at the Plough in George Street? Built in 1833, the Plough was one of the four local pubs that were sacrificed in the name of progress. Back in the 19th century, building regulations were not what they are today; nevertheless the Plough's owner, Richard How, was brought before the magistrates for causing an obstruction with his new building. The old pub was demolished in 1973, but at least some of the fabric of the building was preserved and put on display in Luton museum as part of the public house display.

Milletts has long been a name to be reckoned with in the realm of workwear. Duffle coats, trousers, jackets, shirts, boots, you name it - if it was workwear - and you could almost certainly buy it at Milletts. Stuffed to bursting point with an immense range of goods, this store was the obvious port of call for any bloke who needed either working gear or casual clothes. These buildings were all demolished to make way for the new Barclays Bank (to the left of the photograph) and the Arndale development.

Bottom: Countless Lutonians will undoubtedly remember the Odeon as the scene of their first date, perhaps their first shy kiss in the back row. Others will remember the Saturday matinees of their younger days, usually punctuated by cheers and jeers, flying bits of rubbish, the popping of bubble gum - and the 'oohs' of excitement when The Lone Ranger or Roy Rogers rode into danger. All very thrilling stuff. The Odeon was built in 1938 - the heyday of cinema entertainment - with an amazing capacity of almost 2,000 seats, and champagne and caviare accompanied the grand opening ceremony. The first film to be shown was 'The Drum', which starred the well-known actor Sabu. In 1974 it was converted into a triple-screen cinema. The advent of television was probably the beginning of the end for the Odeon; TV took off in a big way during the 1950s and sadly brought down the final curtain on six of Luton's eight cinemas. The Odeon cinema closed in 1983, and the facility fought valiantly on as a bingo club. In 1997 its new name - The Mecca - brought controversy to the town when a Muslim group raised objections, which were of course settled amicably.

Bottom: This nostalgic view of Manchester Street takes us on a trip down Memory Lane to a scene that has changed almost beyond recognition since it was caught on camera in February 1976. As we look towards the railway bridge and New Bedford Road, the businesses on the right were at the time nearing the end of their life. Soon, Currys electrical business and Walkers Shoes would have to vacate their premises, though the buildings on the left managed to survive when St George's Square was laid down. Though we may regret the passing of so many older properties, at least we can say that if they had to go, St George's Square has made a good replacement, giving Luton an area of open space, trees and green lawns - and a breath of fresh air - right in the middle of the town and overlooked by the magnificent Town Hall.

Right: Remember shopping at Fine Fare supermarket in Dunstable Road? This was March 1962, and sweeping changes in shopping were hitting not only Luton, but towns and cities across the UK. How strange it felt when those first self-service shops opened, to help ourselves from the goods on display on the shelves - it was almost like stealing!

Those small self-service shops led quickly to the opening of the larger supermarkets such as Fine Fare, Sainsbury's and Tesco's. Many smaller grocers went with the popular flow, supplying wire baskets and installing self-service units, but the new trend eventually resulted in the demise of many of Luton's corner shops. Adjacent to Fine Fare is the Luton Greeting Card Centre; we see by the 'Players' advert above the door that you could stock up on cigarettes as well as buy Great Uncle Albert a birthday card. Players have been pleasing smokers since the enduring slogan 'Players Please' appeared back in the 1920s.

Above: It was 1976 when this scene of George Street was caught on camera, and redevelopment was already well underway, with the new Barclays Bank building taking up the right foreground. Financial establishments are well represented in George Street, with Natwest directly opposite Barclays, and the Britannia, the Woolwich, HSBC, the Abbey National and Lloyds TSB assisting Luton's cash flow on either side of the street further along. There was little traffic around in George Street at the time of the photograph, but as the number of

cars in the town centre increased so did the number of accidents. Luton responded by introducing traffic free areas, and George Street was made subsequently converted into a pedestrianised area. Some of us might miss the old town, but parents with prams and young children are especially grateful for the safety of the traffic free street.

Top: The top of Market Hill has long been a pleasant place to sit and contemplate the world - but didn't these benches seem regimented when you compare them with the same spot today? Set one behind the other they seemed almost like cinema seats or church pews. The terraces of today, set well above street level, are easy on the eye and contribute to a varied outlook that is Continental in style; George Street, with its shops, its 'candle-snuffer' booths and its bars, could almost pass for a street scene in Paris! There are a multitude of places nearby where Lutonians and visitors to the town can sit and quench their thirst, and watch the world go by: the Dog and Donut, Brookes Cafe Bar and Yates's Wine Lodge, to name only a few. The photograph was taken in 1962, and the old Barclays Bank still stands on the right of the picture. Further along was Blundells, a favourite department store with many Lutonians.

On the home front

Dib, dib, dib! Cooking in the open air has always been a lot more fun than making meals in the kitchen, and judging by the smiles on the faces of these Girl Guides, they were enjoying this demonstration of their cookery skills as much as today's youngsters enjoy slaving over their veggie-burgers or chicken legs on a hot barbie! The exercise was staged as part of Wings for Victory Week (during the second world war, 'Weeks' were often held to raise funds for one cause or another), and it is thought that the Womens Voluntary Service supervised the event. The ability to organise good hot meals in a wartime emergency was an essential part of the work of the WVS, who, with a membership of well over six thousand, were the largest women's voluntary group in Luton. They undertook a thousand an one tasks that no-one else had the time to do, ranging from taking care of air raid victims and providing hot drinks and snacks from mobile canteens to knitting, sorting clothing, and helping with the children who had been evacuated to Luton.

Below: Slaving over a hot stove was an occupation these members of the Luton Women's Voluntary Service practised in their spare time as well as at home! The WVS was founded to help people in need, and part of their work has always been attending emergencies in peace as well as in wartime. At any time the service has to be ready to cope with full-scale disaster situations, and this involves preparing thousands of cups of tea and huge quantities of food. All this cannot be done, of course, without prior planning and organisation so regular exercises help the members to establish a well-organised system of working. Exercises are still held regularly today, though the venue is more likely to be a school hall or a community centre than a camp under canvas. The old field kitchen equipment has now been packed away - though it is still kept on hand, just in case!

Bottom: We are not aware of what part these cheerful men played in this WVS exercise back in 1956, and the rope knotted around their waists is very intriguing to those who are not in the know! Though all this happened more than 40 years ago, it's possible that some of the men (rather older today!) will be among our readers and will recognise themselves and remember what this was all about.

Developing and teaching skills to serve the community has always been the priority of the WRVS, and exercises ensure that regular women can practise their field skills and learn to cope with large-scale emergencies. They have to learn to utilise any materials that lie to hand, such as building makeshift tables from a few planks of wood with an empty oil drum at each corner. The WRVS still perform vital emergency help; in December 1997 800 homes were evacuated in Cadoxton, South Wales, after a rail tanker carrying toxic chemicals was derailed. In conjunction with other agencies, the WRVS set up rest centres at two leisure centres in Barry to cope with the 160 evacuees (and 18 pets!).

Above: What was afoot at this WVS exercise? We are intrigued by this little gathering of Lutonians - which included a number of gentlemen who were obviously very privileged to be included in this usually female domain. The ladies busily engaged in the inside of the van on the left would have been part of the 'Food Squad' - we can see a couple of their mobile units in the background of this shot, and we can guess that their skills in emergency food preparation are about to be demonstrated. Perhaps free samples and a warming cuppa would have been on offer when the demonstration was over! Cooking was at the time seen as one of those 'jobs for the girls', and when the bombs began to fall during World War II the WVS mobile canteens were a cheering sight to Luton's Civil Defence workers. A hot mug of tea was often just what they needed as they battled with coolness and courage hour after hour in unbelievable conditions to rescue people from their damaged homes.

Right: This photograph is identified as a WVS exercise, and during the second world war

serving food was a key task of this band of capable women. Not only did they run the mobile canteens that brought relief to troops, bomb victims and rescue workers, but they also staffed the Food Emergency Van Service. During World War II many workers were involved in reconstruction jobs that had no canteen facilities and were well away from the town centre. Food was prepared in Luton's British Restaurant and was taken to these isolated sites by WVS workers on a daily basis. Staff for the Civil Defence Canteen and the British Restaurant in New Town Street was also drawn from the ranks of the redoubtable WVS, as was a significant number of helpers in the American Red Cross Club.

Her Majesty the Queen paid tribute to the work of the WVS in 1966 by adding 'Royal' to the title. The agency continue to play a vital role in providing care where needed, and the WRVS today provide an average of 350 meals every day for their 'Meals on Wheels' service. They still run a maternity shop for the benefit of new mothers, situated in the Luton & Dunstable Hospital.

Below: Harvest Festival. The very words conjure up visions of well polished apples heaped up at the front of the church, glowing like rubies, along with piles of home grown potatoes scrubbed free of clinging soil, long, orange-coloured carrots complete with fern-like greenery, leeks, onions, bulbous marrows, golden chrysanthemums, crimson and purple dahlias - and always the odd pumpkin or two, the proud offering from the allotments of those dads who are keen gardeners. Every church, every school, every nursery - all have their own tradition of the 'harvest home', and the produce, a yearly offering begged from parents whether they are gardeners or not, is traditionally distributed to the elderly in the community.

Mrs Hutchinson was the lady on the left of the photograph who in her capacity of Welfare Worker was privileged to bless some of the older residents of Luton from the offerings made at one of the local Harvest Festivals; the box no doubt contained a welcome addition to this lady's diet.

Bottom: These busy members of the Luton branch of the WVS were caught on camera sorting through donations of food made during an appeal for supplies. Jars of jam - no doubt home made from that summer's ripe strawberries, or blackberries gleaned from laneside bushes, take up much of the foreground. No doubt home-pickled onions, chutneys and piccalillies were among the jars too. As the photograph is undated we cannot say whether this was a World War II appeal for those made homeless by bombing raids, or whether the produce was later sold to bring in some much-needed funds for the organisation. We can say, however, that the work of the WVS - today the WRVS - continues to be a much valued part of community life, not only in Luton but across the country. During 1998 they provided 12 million meals on wheels to 100,000 recipients and assisted at 128 real-life emergencies. After the death of Diana, Princess of Wales, the WRVS provided refreshments for people who queued for up to 12 hours to sign the books of condolence. And it was WRVS members who helped to clear up the incredible 25,000 tonnes of flowers after the event.

The WRVS collect and sort over 12,000 garments every year

Sorting, parcelling and sending magazines was part of the work taken on by the WVS, but we are left in the dark as to who the fortunate recipients of this selection of Womans Own, Time and Tide, Vanity Fair and Vogue will be. The names of most of these ladies are, however, known to us: from left to right they are Mrs Coomber, Mrs Johnson, Mrs Fisher, Mrs Cuthbert and Mrs Wheatley. The Women's Royal Voluntary Service, as it is today, continues to depend heavily on the generosity of others, in the giving of time and skills as well as in financial donations. Collecting and sorting around 12,000 garments every year, supplying a Meals on Wheels service to the elderly, supporting needy families, supplying voluntary drivers for those who are not able, for one reason and another, to use public transport, along with a multitude of other tasks, have long identified the role of this wonderful organisation.

On the move

Below: Where were these happy day-trippers bound for? Perhaps they were off to sample the delights of London for the day, to marvel at the Tower, gaze in awe at London Bridge, or embark on the real adventure of a boat trip down the Thames. We will never know, but the atmosphere of relaxation, of looking forward to a great day out, can be seen in the eager smiles on the faces of these holiday-makers - interestingly, made up entirely of women and children. We have no date for this photograph, but the fashions are those of the 1940s, and ankle strap shoes, padded shoulders and just-below-the-knee hemlines were worn by the ladies, while at least one of the children still wears the hair ribbon that was popular among little girls born in the 40s. Few families owned cars before post-war prosperity became a reality, and day trips such as this one were a rare treat to be looked forward to for weeks beforehand.

Bottom: Personal attention at a filling station...those were the days! Long gone, sadly, though more mature readers will remember with nostalgia the time when you could drive your car into a petrol station and not only have the services of attendants who filled up your tank, but who also cleaned your windscreen and asked if you needed oil. This particular filling station was Shaw and Kilburn's Vauxhall garage in Dunstable Road, and

especially interesting is the wide selection of brand names and types of petrol that were on offer there. As well as two kinds of Esso (wasn't Esso Ethyl an alcohol based fuel?), Shell, National and Cleveland Discol provided an alternative choice. We have no date for the photograph, but as two of the attendants in the picture are female we can conclude that some ladies were finding jobs that would take them away from the kitchen sink and give them a degree of independence. These girls, however, would be more likely to be petrol attendants than mechanics; the days when females would encroach on the widespread 'jobs for the boys' attitude still lay far in the future.

Above: The 1950s saw the beginning of post-war prosperity and the advent of the package holiday, giving a boost to Britain's tour operators in general and Luton Airport in particular. With a calculating eye to the future, a new concrete runway was planned and built in 1959, giving the Airport an extra five and a half thousand feet of runway (later extended to eight thousand feet). By 1961, when this photograph was taken, a total of £225,662 had been invested in improving the facilities at Luton Airport. The end of the decade saw nearly 420,000 travellers passing through Luton - and the total rose year by year until the mid 1970s. The impressive aircraft waiting on the apron for its passengers to board is a DC3 Dakota, one of the most successful civilian aircraft ever built. A number of Dakotas are still operated in Britain by Air Atlantique (based in Coventry), though today their operations are largely confined to oil spillage work and pleasure flights.

This photograph might be carefully arranged and rather stiffly posed to show the staff at their very best, yet it allows us a glimpse back through time to the passenger lounge of the old terminal building at Luton Airport, and more than one reader will exclaim 'I remember it when it looked like that'. At the time, of course, this was a brand new facility - albeit a temporary one - that Luton could be justifiably proud of - the terminal building it replaced had been a simple wooden hut. The light and airy lounge was all mod cons, with tea, coffee and snacks on offer, along with a waiting area where passengers could wait for their flight in comfort. The building of the M1 brought further business to Luton, and the beginning of the 1960s saw the airport facilities extended all round, with the installation of an identity beacon, a new radar system, and more than 1,000 feet of new approach lights.

Left: Few of today's travellers would recognise this virtually deserted scene as Luton International Airport in its early years! The aircraft standing on the otherwise empty apron is thought to be an Auster high wing monoplane; are these two men the aeroplane's pilot and passenger? We have no date for this photograph, but we do know that this new control tower was completed in September 1952 and was officially opened by A T Lennox-Boyd, representing the Ministry of Transport and Aviation. The new facility had everything that was state-of-the-art in the early 1950s, with a meteorological room, records department, generation equipment, up to date offices and of course the nerve centre of the operation - the control room. The airport's reception area took up much of the ground floor. Luton's customs facility was re-installed as part of the airport's improvements - an asset to incoming travellers who had formerly had to stop off at Southampton to be cleared through customs.

Above: Vauxhall Motors have come a very long way since they produced their very first car in London in 1903! That particular car would have set you back £136, and though it possessed a two-speed gearbox and had no reverse gear, the new car - cheaper to keep on the road than the average horse - became a popular mode of transport. Vauxhall's became a success story, and within a mere 50 years their output had topped 100,000 vehicles a year - an achievement that coincided with their Golden Jubilee in 1953. By 1957 there were an impressive 22,000 employees on the payroll.

This view, taken from the car park, gives us a glimpse of how Vauxhall's Luton works had developed by 1962. The success of the Victor (which in the 1950s became Britain's number one export car), the Wyvern, the Velox and the Cresta is legendary; in 1962 you could buy a new Velox for just over £900, while the more luxurious Cresta cost around £80 more.

Shopping spree

An accident involving an LMS dray, and the drama has drawn a crowd of onlookers to the scene in George Street. The photograph raises more questions than it answers, however. We cannot see whether any other vehicle was involved, we don't know exactly what happened - and we are not sure whether anyone was hurt in the incident (though judging by the size of the crowd we might conclude that the unlucky carter lies somewhere on the other side of the dray). And what happened to the poor old horse that had been drawing the cart? Sadly, we will never know all the facts. The load piled high on the dray includes a number of wooden hat crates; there were many hat factories in George Street at that time. The accident happened right outside Burton's gents' outfitters; we have no date for the photograph, but we know that this scene took place before 1938, when the Savoy Cinema was built on the site of this building.

'Great Clearance Sale!' shouts the notice in the window of the Luton Industrial Co-operative Society, and at least one customer is eagerly scanning the goods on display as she looks for a bargain. This, as the sign on the corner of the building informs us, was Luton Co-op's Number One branch; when it was first opened in 1897 the shop was considerably less ornate than it was at the time of the photograph.

The Co-operative movement started more than a century ago in Rochdale, where a group of local weavers found 28 people who were willing to pay £1 each to buy goods and open a shop. Customers were awarded a dividend on everything they bought. The idea caught on in a big way, and eventually there were enough societies to have their own suppliers.

Beginning with footwear, soap and biscuits the Co-operative Wholesale Society began to manufacture its own goods, provide insurance and arrange affordable funerals. A revealing sign on the side of the building tells passers-by that Co-operative products were 'manufactured by the people for the people'.

Plait Halls - to find the best - and cheapest - apples, pears, oranges, grapefruit and bananas. Buying tomatoes and cucumber from one stall, apples and sprouts from another and perhaps potatoes and a couple of grapefruit from a third have always been part of the fun of bargain hunting in the market.

Top: Luton has had a long succession of different markets in its history, and this nostalgic photograph, taken on 14th July 1968, will bring back a lot of happy memories of many enjoyable shopping hours! The facility opened

Above: The old covered market had an atmosphere of its very own, didn't it? The subtle scents of oranges and apples competing with the sharper odours of onions and leeks.... You could buy more than fruit and vegetables in Luton Market, however - this was the place to buy anything from a book to a bag.

The well-stocked fruit stalls would have made a good starting place for a lot of Lutonian housewives, who week after week would catch a bus into town and tour the market - which in earlier days had been the

in 1925, though originally it was one of the two Plait Halls that formed an essential part of the town's tradition hat making industry.

The prices charged by markets and street traders have traditionally been a few coppers cheaper than the average high street greengrocer would charge, and a weekly tour of the market stalls could save a shilling or two here and there, and stretch the inadequate housekeeping money a little bit further. Sadly, the facility closed in December 1972. Today, the market is housed in the Arndale Centre.

Office life as it used to be - and not a computer in sight! Computers did not exist, in fact, when this view of the Skefco Ball Bearing Company's office was caught for posterity by the photographer. Unfortunately the photograph is undated, and even close examination of the calendar hanging on the window frame fails to reveal a year - though we can see that the month was May. At the time, Skefco's workforce numbered more than 1,000, and the company were well on their way to becoming the second largest employer in the Luton area. All this spelled a lot of paperwork, stored not on disk but in neatly stacked files and ledgers. Typewriters such as the one in the background were the latest technology - and they were built to last. Thousands of these wonderful machines are still in working order and still in use, in spite of the popularity of the word processor! Spot the telephone being used by the clerk on his feet in the background. Today, a visit to SKF's website will provide you with a comprehensive history of the company from its early beginnings in Sweden back in 1907.

At work

Below: Maurice Chevalier, eat your heart out! Straw boaters by the hundred - at a guess, all being crated ready to be sent to the retailer. The presence of a number of children in the photograph is a bit of a mystery, though we must bear in mind that as youngsters left school far earlier at the time, they could have been apprentices. Luton's traditional hat industry was established in the area by the 17th century using locally-grown straw plait; by 1900 hat manufacture was at its peak in the town. Unfortunately, hat making ebbs and flows with the vagaries of fashion, and as the wearing of hats went into decline so did the industry, and by the 1930s engineering had taken over as Luton's number one employer. As straw boaters and straw school hats went out of fashion, however, Luton's hat manufacturers turned their attention to felt hat manufacture, and though many of the original buildings have been demolished (a great number disappeared beneath the Arndale), the 'hatters quarter' conservation area was set up in Luton in 1991.

Ball bearings, Swedish style!

It is hardly surprising that Luton has twinned with the Swedish town Eskilstuna rather than the run of the mill, closer to home, towns favoured by many councils. Since 1910 SKF, formerly Skefko, has been a major force in the growth and prosperity of Luton and, as every local schoolboy knows, SKF started in Sweden. Dr Sven Wingquist, pioneer of the double row self-aligning ball bearing, founded the company in the fine old seaport city of Gothenburg in 1907.

At the time, horse-drawn road vehicles were able to cope with friction by packing their axles with thick grease, but this age-old remedy was no match for the high speeds and intense heats generated by industrial machinery. Steam ships and railway engines too were hampered by the need to control friction between their moving parts - as were the new, ungainly, variably reliable and exciting motor cars bought by the wealthy.

SKF is derived from the initial letters of Dr Wingquist's company which set out to remedy the problem shared by all machine builders and operators. As demand from manufacturers in England was

Left: *Dr Sven Wingquist, who founded the company in Gothenburg in 1907.*
Below: *Female workers at the turn of the century.*
Bottom: *TH Dryden, who together with Tinsley Waterhouse, took over the reins of the company in England.*

It was registered in 1910 under the name The Skefko Ball Bearing Company Ltd and commenced work with 150 staff in 1911, King George V's coronation year. 180 bearings a day made from imported Swedish steel was the average production during the first year. Next year the offices in London were transferred to Luton, where the Luton News commented 'The coming of this new industry to Luton is likely to be of supreme value to the town as the years go by......Electric light is used (gas light was still the norm), and the men have a mess-room....to have their meals in comfort.'

SKF has always kept up to date - from the days when electricity was as revolutionary as the provision of decent facilities for the staff, to the present. The first tram to use Skefko bearings was tried out in the hilly city of Sheffield, the City of Steel, in 1912. After three years running at a loss the company made a profit and set out to expand by building an extension and appointing agents in London, Birmingham and Manchester at home. Foreign agencies were also established in India, Canada and the Union of South Africa.

By that fateful August in 1914, Skefko employed 250 who produced 3,500 bearings a week in an enlarged factory. During the Great War, the company enjoyed priority in the delivery of essential raw materials.

steadily growing the three year old company bought land on the edge of the old hat making town of Luton to be the home of their first overseas factory. Foreign investment in English skills is nothing new and the sum of £30,000 was estimated as sufficient to get the factory started.

Above left: *The employees in the early 1900s.*
Top: *Factory workers.*

Production continued to rise as the factory was enlarged again to twice its original size in the fields bought in anticipation of growth. The Swedish parent firm sent finished bearings as well as steel to Luton to supply the enormous wartime demand. Dr Wingquist celebrated his fortieth birthday in 1916 and next year the Luton staff enjoyed their first works outing to nearby Woburn Sands.

By 1918 all the components of the bearings, that is the rings, the steel balls or rollers and the cages, were made in the Luton factory where there were then 775 staff producing 24,000 bearings a month. The company's first Social and Sports Club was opened but such was the limitation on space that many of the early athletic events were run in the factory yard. Improved production methods almost doubled production in the first year of peace as ball bearings were here to stay; this was no wartime flash in the pan expansion.

The Roaring Twenties was an amazing era for those who had grown up in the staid days of Queen Victoria and the Edwardian Summer which followed. Public motor buses and horse drawn drays alike were fitted with Skefko bearings to reduce friction and increase productivity - in the case of horses, by 30 percent. Growth was stunted by the post war depression, despite several royal visits, which affected most industries including vital suppliers like Skefko. Everyone from tea boys to directors endured reduced salaries so that the firm could continue to employ as many of its loyal staff as possible during the difficult years between 1921-26 when the motto was 'Hold On'.

Taper and cylindrical roller bearings came off the lines at Luton as the employees numbered 1,000 and the slogan 'The right bearing in the right place' hit the hoardings.

The company Tennis Club was formed with members taking responsibility for preparing and laying out two hard courts. The winners and runners up of the famous Isle of Man TT Races all rode British motor cycles using Skefko bearings, well known marques such as Douglas, New Gerrard, HRD, Cotton, Norton, New Imperial and the Rex Acme.

The independent railway companies, some 100 years old, were beginning to fit their rolling stock with roller bearing axleboxes. The 1920s pioneers of international flying found Skefko bearings as good as new after inter-continental flights and a Bentley fitted with Skefko bearings won the Le Mans motor race. Amy Johnson's de Havilland Tiger Moth flew to Australia with Skefko bearings, as did the beautiful Schneider Trophy winner from which the Spitfire was developed. 'Big Peter' at York Minster, one of the largest bells in England was rehung with Skefko bearings after which

Above: *The Capstan Lathe section in the 1920s.*
Below: *Staff in the 1920s.*

Skefko enjoyed improving trade and introduced a narrow spherical roller bearing with a loose flange guide. The factory girls of the time were outfitted in natty overalls which reflected the current taste for the balloon topped jodhpur style trousers worn by seaside Pierettes. Heavy industry in India was so increasing its demand for Skefko products that the branch office in India became a subsidiary of the Swedish firm.

Skefko celebrated its Silver Jubilee in time with King George V in 1935 and marked its twenty-fifth anniversary by putting up a brand new canteen capable of holding seven hundred at a sitting. The Foremens' Dinner was a formal well dressed affair as expected in the days when qualified craftsmen wore ties on the factory floor. The Luton News reported that Skefko bearings were used on the railways of fifty three countries. The year 1936 was marked, not only by the world's first television broadcast from London, but by SKF offering 50 percent of the Skefko shares to the British public and staff numbers in Luton rising to 2,000. Further expansion was allowed for by the purchase of 44 acres at Sundon some two and a half miles from the Leagrave Road site.

The year 1937 was a record breaking twelve months for Skefko in which plans for company sports fields were introduced at the same time as staff pensions and life assurance schemes were set up. The year was also marked by the coronation of the shy Duke of York as King George VI and the appointment of SKF's Chairman as Swedish Ambassador to the English Court of St James. A fire in the packing department spread quickly but

it moved so easily that a single bell ringer could turn it with one hand.

Production continued to increase as more and more manufacturers fitted Skefko bearings into their machine tools and products enabling the company to reduce its prices. The palatial stair hall and other appointments in the main office block reflected the burgeoning success of a firm providing vital components in the Machine Age. A race was run between the fabulous train de luxe 'Le Train Bleu' and a Rover car, both equipped with Skefko bearings, from the Cote d'Azur to Calais, which was won by a twenty minutes lead on indifferent roads by the car! The twenties had style!

Following the ups and downs of the twenties, which ended with the Wall Street crash, the thirties got off to a rotten start. In spite of the international depression

Above left: The turning department.
Top: The sales room.

thanks to the company firemen and Luton Fire Brigade it was brought under control within four hours of starting. The opening of new sports facilities at the Sundon site was balanced by more war-like preparations as the clouds of war loomed over the last years of the decade.

Skefko was asked to participate in the defence of the nation by placing its technical expertise and production at the disposal of HM Government, at last awake to the threat of war. The time won by the Munich Treaty enabled Britain to prepare for the second world war. Skefko set up a Civil Defence unit which trained in fire fighting and the evacuation and care of civilians under aerial attack. The much extended factory was cleverly disguised, not only by painted camouflage but with a fake road and trees travelling across the factory roofs to confuse bomber pilots searching for known targets.

Production was maintained, and then increased, by stock piling steel and recruiting staff from outside Luton. The Ministry of Economic Warfare caused freighters to make the risky voyage from Sweden bringing material to be transformed into the sinews of mechanised warfare. These were deployed at sea, in the air, in land fighting machines and in transport enterprises and factories alike. The company formed its own Home Guard company to provide day and night sentries while work mates made over a quarter of a

million bearings every week. Visits by royalty and government ministers helped to encourage a people at war in the desperate days when vital components were ferried from Sweden in super fast naval MTBs and RAF Mosquito aircraft.

Peace was celebrated by everyone in Britain enjoying an extra two days holiday before slogging it out, under the harsh slogan 'Work or Want', as Britain struggled to pay off immense war loans. Battered factories, beset by rationing of all supplies, attempted to regain peace time

Below: HRH The Duchess of Kent with the chairman during her visit to Skefko in 1943.
Bottom: An annual staff dinner in the early 1950s.

markets while Skefko continued to turn out bearings for a world busy repairing the damage of six lost years. The late forties were marked by the joyful and colourful Royal Wedding, a national fuel crisis and Dior's glamourous New Look. The incredible Bristol Brabazon air liner, though decades ahead of its time and with its engines fitted with Skefko bearings, was not a success.

Many of the staff who celebrated a quarter of a century with the company received awards for their long service while the new 'Get Well' scheme paid for Skefko staff to convalesce at Langton Hall Hotel in sunny Bournemouth. The 1951 Festival of Britain provided Skefko with a wonderful advertising showcase as the company improved both its production facilities and its pension schemes. HM Queen's coronation year in 1953 saw further developments at Skefko including the

purchase of 90 acres of land and the subsequent growth of the technical department. Neighbouring farmers no doubt set themselves up for retirement on the proceeds.

Skefko's Golden Jubilee in 1960 followed the equipping of the massive Jodrell Bank space telescope with SKF bearings and the building of another works canteen as part of an eighty-fold increase on the original works floor area. Since then a Skefko factory in Ayrshire came and went in eighteen years, a sure sign of changing times, while, in 1973, Skefko changed its name to SKF (U.K.) Ltd. The Seventies also saw the Sheffield Twist Drill and Steel Co. acquired by SKF, another temporary diversification, while in 1977, HM Queen's Jubilee year, all production in Luton moved to the Sundon works.

The eighties were marked by the formation of SKF Engineering Products to take advantage of business opportunities in other fields which led to the development of SKF (UK) Service Ltd. This organisation builds on SKF's long established reputation in the field of advising world wide customers on the selection and employment of SKF products best suited to their needs. Since then SKF has developed ceramic bearings as an alternative to steel for use in high-tech equipment such as the first supersonic car, the amazing 764mph Thrust SSC. Dr Wingquist would no doubt have said 'Kolossal', or even 'Skaal', to developments which keep his invention to the fore in an ever faster changing world.

One can hardly be surprised that a firm with a long record of treating its staff decently should win the 1995 Investors in People Award for the Industrial Division and has since gone on to receive environmental plaudits with ISO 14001 recognition. Remember the 'supreme value to the town' comment in the Luton News of 1912.

Above: *The factory today.*
Left: *SKF Industrial Division won Investors in People status in 1995.*

Powering towards the next millennium

Through the centuries, intelligent observation of the behaviour of water in its various states and the subsequent development of applications based on these observations has led to a number of invaluable inventions. To cite just a few examples: Archimedes, we are told, noticed that the level of his bathwater rose when he got in, cried, 'Eureka!' and went on to develop the Archimedes principle; the behaviour of the domestic hot-water kettle inspired James Watt to invent a steam engine; and Joseph Bramah, working from similar observations, changed the face of industry by inventing the steam press.

Joseph Bramah also invented continuous carbonation and the water closet, and many of his inventions were turned to practical use by his student William Russell, who in 1815 founded a business in St John's Street in the City of London, manufacturing water closets, hydraulic presses and soda water machines. William Russell died in 1835 and his company was taken over by Hayward Tyler, whose family had begun trading in 1783 as tea urn manufacturers. In 1837 Mr Tyler moved his new company to premises in nearby Whitecross Street. Here the manufacture of soda water machines continued, with a patent taken out in

1840, and the brass foundry side of the business developed too; screw-down cocks and various brasswork items for use in the plumbing trade were introduced at this time and remained on the company's catalogue for the next hundred years. In 1855 the company changed hands again; Hayward Tyler died and his widow sold the the firm to a relative, Robert Luke Howard, for £7,500. Robert Howard was himself an engineer who had served his apprenticeship with Messrs Fowler and Fry of Bristol, and the young man brought his own ideas to the company; new products added to the list during the next few decades included such diverse items as machinery for making aerated bread, and the Universal Pump, a single-cylinder steam pump with internal valve gear which was introduced in 1869 and superseded the Direct Acting Pump. Robert's youngest brother Eliot had joined the firm in 1863, and to cope with expansion some adjoining cowsheds had been purchased in 1866 and converted into a new workshop; but the business carried on expanding, and Whitecross

Above: *A Double Suction Hot Oil Pump for oil refinery duties.* ***Below:*** *The machine shop circa 1960.*

Street offered no scope for further enlargement of the premises. The decision was taken to buy land out of London, and a good site was found in a little village, to the north of London, which in 1872 was just beginning to develop as an industrial centre: Luton.

Retaining the London premises as Head Office, the company built a new factory on land near the Great Northern Railway in Luton. With various members of the Howard family investing in the venture, Hayward Tyler became the largest company in Luton at that time, and in fact before the end of the century its workforce was to be instrumental in the formation of the Luton Co-operative Society. The company began to take on Government contracts, building packing presses and in 1878 producing a hay pressing plant for Woolwich Dockyard; that same year the Rider hot air engine was produced, probably at the instigation of one of the firm's American associates, Mr Benson. By that time Robert Samuel Lloyd, a cousin of Robert and Eliot Howard, had also joined the firm, subsequently becoming a partner and playing an important

pioneering role, especially in the development of electrical applications. He assisted in designing and carrying out an experimental installation of Edison's electric light on Holborn Viaduct, and his contributions had a tremendous influence on the design and construction of electrically-driven pumping machinery, waterworks installations, and pumps for pipe-lines and tank vessels. It was partly as a result of Robert Samuel Lloyd's interest that Hayward Tyler took up and developed Mr Edison's invention, becoming the country's original pioneers of conduit wiring, before abandoning electrical contracting in 1905. In 1887 the company created history by fitting electric light and tanker pumps to the 'Robert Dickinson'; this was the first time a tanker had been fitted with such equipment. Another major nautical contract was the fitting the tank steamer 'Vindobala' with one of Hayward Tyler's direct acting steam pumps in 1888; this type of pump was superseded two years later, however, by the Gordon Duplex Pump.

Above: *Gear pump sub assembly.*

Hayward Tyler's imagination and innovation in developing new products was matched by its readiness to embrace new working practices. A private telephone between London and Luton was installed in 1890, representing the ultimate in advanced technology. Hayward Tyler was also one of the first firms in London to install a typewriter, thus becoming one of Remington's oldest customers; but surely the most radical move of all was the appointment of a lady typist to work in the London office!

In 1891 the company purchased land adjoining its existing site and constructed a new iron foundry. By this time the next generation was ready to take their place in the family firm; Henry Fox Howard, Robert's eldest son, was taken into partnership in 1892, and seven years later Eliot's eldest son Francis Eliot Howard also became a partner. Expansion then continued with the acquisition, in 1900, of the Universal Water Meter Company; with this came a contract from the New River Company of London for making plumbers' fittings. The beginning of the 20th century saw more administrative changes when the company sold its London premises in Whitecross Street to Whitbreads, the brewers; the works were not finally closed until 1904, however. The partnership then set up offices at 99 Queen Victoria Street, becoming a private limited company the

Above: *A view of the Hayward Tyler factory main machine shop.*

following year with Robert Luke Howard as Chairman, Eliot Howard as Secretary and the other partners as directors. In 1915 - a hundred years after the founding of the company - Robert was succeeded as Chairman by Eliot. In spite of losing his sight during the middle years of his life, Robert Luke Howard had headed this successful Company for 60 years. He died in 1919 at the age of 85.

In Luton, meanwhile, disaster had struck. When the factory there had been under construction, many difficulties had been encountered in obtaining the ironwork needed for the frames of the various structures. In the end, timber had to be used instead in many cases, and one of the buildings where timber was used for the roof frame was the large Engineers' Shop. For 30 years or so this proved perfectly satisfactory, but on the evening of 23rd October 1903 a spark from a passing train happened to drift in through a

louvre in the roof, to settle on some wood patterns stored in the East Gallery, which then ignited. Fortunately some men were working late that evening, and they rang the factory bell to summon the Town Fire Brigade. Unfortunately, however, despite the best efforts of the Fire Brigade and the works' own steam pump and fire appliances, it was not possible to extinguish the blaze once it had spread to the roof timbers. Nor was it possible to remove the machinery which stood inside the Engineers' Shop. All that could be done was prevent the fire from spreading to adjoining premises, while inevitably the blazing roof of the Engineers' Shop eventually collapsed, causing damage to plant and machinery estimated at £50,000. This was a severe blow to the company, particularly since the loss was by no means covered by insurance. It was also at first seen as potentially disastrous by many of the company's employees, who feared that they would be left, at least temporarily, without a job. In fact the company did all it could to keep the men working. They were all engaged in clearing up the debris and then in setting up temporary working arrangements, and as a result the company was able to safeguard the men's pay and keep disruption to its customers to a minimum. One development which was lost for ever in the fire, however, was an embryonic prototype of the first automobile in Luton; this was still in the early developmental stages when it was destroyed, and the project was never resumed.

The firm's first major innovation as a limited company came in 1908, when one of its employees, W R McDonald, succeeded in insulating an electric motor effectively enough, by winding it with rubber coated cable, for it to be operated underwater; this development was incorporated into Hayward Tyler's marine salvage pumps. The Admiralty was the chief customer for these pumps, and some years later they were used to refloat the German warships sunk at Scapa Flow during the first world war.

Left: Glandless boiler circulating pump.
Below: Submersible motors on assembly.

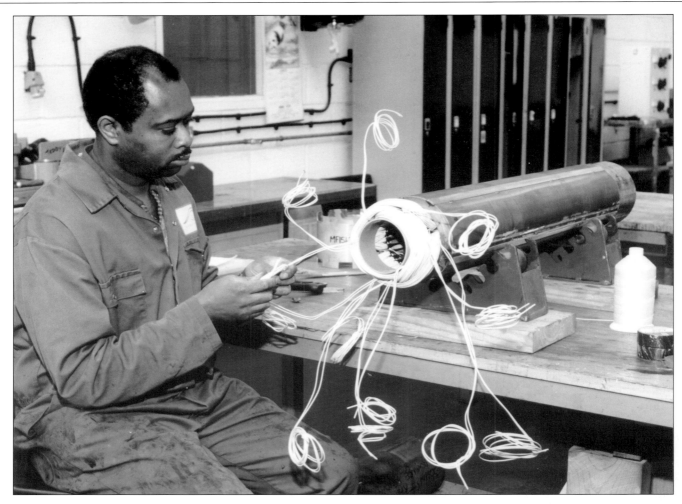

During the first world war Hayward Tyler was placed upon the Admiralty Vital List and was called upon to manufacture a range of essential components. For a time the company was sole supplier for machined engine fittings and cast engine sumps for Churchill tanks. They were also contracted to provide 75 milling machines for the Ministry of Supply, five steam engines for Admiralty barges, 40 pumps for Operation Pluto, 70 sets of submersible borehole pumps for emergency water supply, and 1,750 small pumps for the No. 7 Predictor. During the five years of conflict, 250,000 Oerlikon and automatic gun parts and breech mechanisms were manufactured. Extra staff were employed on the war work. Fortunately none of those working in the factory during the war was killed, although the company's premises suffered badly, being hit first by two bombs during the very first air raid on Luton, on 30th August 1940, and then further damaged by landmines in a night raid a fortnight later. The old Brass Foundry Pattern Stores were completely demolished in the first incident, and in the second the Foundry was damaged; overall the loss amounted to some £3,000.

Once the war was over the Company began to reassess its position and look to the future. It planned to increase the output of mineral water machinery, and additional premises near Edinburgh were leased for this purpose. The company also arranged a special dinner in December 1946 for its many long-serving employees. Eighty-seven employees and ex-employees gathered together, all of whom had completed at least 45 years' service; the average age of the men was calculated to be over 70, and their combined service to the

Company well over 4,000 years! The oldest employee was 75-year-old Mr Cokayne, who had worked for Hayward Tyler for 60 years.

Such staff loyalty must be proof of a company's caring attitude towards its employees. Hayward Tyler's workforce particularly appreciated the Company's policy of joint consultation, which meant that everybody was kept

Above: *A sub-sea submersible motor.*
Top: *Submersible motors rewinding process.*

informed of the Company's financial position and was involved in decision-making. Staff development was also high on the Company's list of priorities. A full-time Training or Education Officer was employed, and training programmes were in place from as early as the first half of the 20th century, with all boys who joined the firm straight from school being given the opportunity of organised training. Their progress was reviewed when they reached the age of 18, and those who showed particular promise were given the chance of becoming student apprentices, which was designed to equip them for an executive post.

During the mid-1900s the output of the Luton factory was divided into four product groups: oil pumps, Duplex steam and power driven pumps, submersible borehole and de-watering pumps, and machinery for bottling mineral water. Many of the large pumps were destined for use in mines and water supply, and Hayward-Tyler was responsible for the manufacture of the world's largest submersible motorised pump at that time, developing 400 horse power and built for export to a mine in Malaya for use in de-watering. Hayward Tyler has exported in excess of 20,000 centrifugal

process pumps to more than 50 countries for many arduous hot and cold oil applications. Another Hayward Tyler innovation was the glandless boiler circulating pump, which is still widely utilised in power generation plants; Hayward Tyler has remained the world's number one supplier of this item and has more recently adapted the pump for the assisted circulation waste heat recovery boiler market.

Today, applications in mining and water supply have been superseded by the ever-developing needs of the offshore oil and gas industries. Hayward Tyler Engineered Products Ltd's modern design technology means that pumping and drive systems can be easily adapted to meet individual applications, which include sea water lift and fire-fighting. With many of its motors and pumps still operational after 25 years' use, the Company's products have a reputation for reliability even in adverse operating conditions. A range of process pumps, submersible pumps and steam turbines are designed and manufactured by Hayward Tyler & Process Ltd for general industrial use.

Industrial processes will continue to evolve and there will always be scope for new specialised power units. One recent example is a large submersible motor designed and manufactured by Hayward Tyler Engineered Products Ltd. This unit, when complete, will be the largest submersible motor ever manufactured at 3,300HP, operating sub-sea at a depth of 4,000ft. Hayward Tyler's innovative approach to problem solving, combined with its vast accumulation of knowledge of submersible pump and motor design, will ensure that it retains its position at the head of this exciting and specialised industry.

*Left: An aerial view of the Luton premises. **Below:** Hayward Tyler provide thousands of pump units for the Petro-chemical industry.*

Helping people to say 'goodbye'

Neville Funeral Service Limited can trace its origins back to 1875, when brothers Thomas and Edward Neville set up in business together. One of the traditional skills upon which the funeral profession was founded is that of joinery, and by 1875 Thomas and Edward were fully skilled joiners. Their training had followed the usual pattern of those times; they had been apprenticed by their father to a Bedfordshire builder, and having served their apprenticeships they had then gained experience by working as journeymen joiners before setting up shop in their first business premises, at 60 Castle Street, Luton.

The brothers put their joinery skills to a variety of uses. One area of activity which was expanding rapidly in Luton at that time was the building trade. In the course of a decade during which Thomas and Edward Neville founded their business, Luton's population increased by over a third, rising from 17,316 in 1871 to 23,955 in 1881. The growing population needed somewhere to live, so builders were under tremendous pressure to put up new housing. Nevilles helped meet this demand by not only supplying large quantities of cased frames and staircases to other local builders, but also by building a number of houses themselves. Once the new inhabitants and their families had established themselves in Luton, other markets developed, so the Neville brothers also turned their attentions to the other branches of joinery, and to funeral directing.

Soon the brothers acquired the yard at the rear of 60 Castle Street, where they had their stables, cart sheds and storage space for timber, which would have including supplies of the solid elm and oak used to manufacture coffins. It was common practice at the time for craftsmen to live and work at the same

Below: *An early Shellabier and pair outside the Victoria Street premises at the turn of the 20th century.*

address. Many hat manufacturers had their hat factories at the rear of their dwellings, and Thomas and Edward Neville adopted this practice in 1892, retaining their existing yard for stabling and storage but setting up a new workshop at number 30 Castle Street, where they also had their living accommodation. The company was to retain joinery workshops at this address for three-quarters of a century, although as can be imagined the original two-level shop and mill, with its gas engines and belt drives, underwent considerable modification during that period!

Thomas and Edward Neville took on their first apprentice in 1881. The signed indenture is still in existence today, and the terms and conditions of employment to which Arthur Cawdell agreed might come as a shock to some of today's Modern Apprentices. Not only did he undertake to serve his masters faithfully, keep their secrets, and gladly do their lawful commands, he also promised not to get married during his apprenticeship, not to play dice or cards, not to haunt taverns, and not to absent himself day or night. He worked a fifty-hour week, ten hours each weekday except Saturday, and his starting pay was three shillings a week (15 pence in

today's currency), rising to eight shillings a week (40 new pence) by the end of his apprenticeship.

T & E Neville were joined around the turn of the 20th century by Stanley Henman, a foreman-joiner from Bromham, near Bedford. Stanley Henman's knowledge and skill contributed a great deal to the company's growing reputation for high-class joinery; and in 1906 the association between the two families was further strengthened when he married Thomas Neville's daughter Clara.

In 1909 Thomas Neville's son, known as 'Tom Junior', joined the company. The aspect of the business which interested him the most was funeral directing. When he became responsible for the Funeral Service, he established a coach yard and stables in buildings in Victoria Street which the company acquired for this purpose. The funeral fleet at that time comprised a dozen black Belgian horses, two glass-sided hearses and four Shellabiers. Tom Junior continued to develop the Funeral Service, while at the same time playing a very active

Above: *An early invoice for a funeral.*
Top: *Staff assembled in the Castle Street yard in 1919.*

E. NEVILLE,
UILDERS
AND
TRACTORS,
TLE STREET, LUTON.

part in local affairs. He became a Councillor for Luton and was held in great esteem by the people of the town. It was a great blow to his family, to the business and to the local people when he died at an early age in 1930.

Tom Junior was survived for some years by both his father and his uncle; Edward Neville died in 1938, while Thomas reached the age of 94, having continued to take an active interest in the company until his death in 1950. The second world war had disrupted the normal activities of the business, with Stanley Henman keeping the company going, helped by a total workforce of just over 50 who were called upon to build air-raid shelters, repair bomb damage and alter or maintain factories for the war effort. After the war Stanley and Clara's son Bernard, who had originally joined T & E Neville in 1932, returned from active service and started to build the company up again, with one section of the company concentrating on building, and the Funeral Service once more being run as a separate concern.

Between 1950 and 1999 the company has seen a number of changes. The Castle Street premises,

Above: *The Foundation Stone ceremony for Luton Public Library - built by Neville's in 1909.*

which had been the firm's home for 75 years, were scheduled for demolition in 1967 to make way for a section of Luton's new ring road. Fortunately, the company had already purchased Common Farm at Leagrave, thinking that this site would provide additional space for the storage and maintenance of the range of mechanical plant which was being increasingly used by the building section. In the event, the whole company moved to Leagrave, where new offices and workshops were constructed adjacent to the plant yard.

At Leagrave, Neville Funeral Service Limited has continued to extend the range of benefits available to clients. The last decade in particular has brought many changes in the way funerals are arranged and executed. Some families continue to find comfort in the traditional, time-honoured form of the funeral service; however, in recent years less formal, more personalised burial arrangements have become acceptable, and some people prefer to take advantage of the different possibilities to find their own unique way of saying their farewells. Neville Funeral Service has moved with the changing times, offering a traditional but flexible approach and giving their clients a choice. Whether the client chooses a traditional Christian burial, a non-religious service, a woodland burial, or one of the many other options, they can rely on Neville Funeral Service's experience and expertise to deliver the very highest quality of service.

The move to Leagrave gave Neville Funeral Service the opportunity to incorporate new amenities into its premises, and the company has continued to improve the level of facilities so that a high level of comfort is provided for clients. Neville Funeral Service believes that its future is dependent on the standard of its training today, so the training and development of young people in the crafts and skills of the industry has become a company tradition. Neville Funeral Service ensures that its own staff receive full training in the many different skills required by the funeral director of today.

A specialised service which Neville Funeral Service offers is that of repatriation. Bedfordshire's population includes a significant proportion of families who have settled here but whose roots lie overseas, perhaps as a result of their ancestors coming here as migrant workers several generations ago. Neville Funeral Service has organised repatriation to Ireland, India, Pakistan and many other parts of the world.

Neville Funeral Service does not confine itself to funeral directing, but is also involved in the many other aspects of bereavement. On a practical level, the firm can provide memorials and floral tributes, which are produced on its own premises. Should the client so wish, the firm will also take care of the catering arrangements, either at the client's home or on its own premises. But in addition to performing practical services such as these, which many customers find invaluable at a time when they themselves have no desire to attend to practicalities, Neville Funeral Service also assists mourners to come to terms with their bereavement. The firm has established strong links with other bereavement-related organisations in the area, such as Cruse, Sands and Hospice at Home, and deals on a regular basis with the various local hospitals, nursing homes and hospices. As an extension of the company's own training programme, Neville assists with the training of volunteers in some of the bereavement-related organisations, and is also regularly called upon by local churches to give talks and lectures on various aspects of funeral directing.

Below: *A traditional funeral.*

Peter Aspinall, Managing Director of Neville Funeral Service, believes that one way to lessen the trauma of death is for people to formulate and express their wishes with regard to their own funerals before the end of their life approaches. Funeral arrangements can then be made which represent the wishes of the deceased and those who are left. Peter is a strong advocate of pre-arranging funerals, and has in fact written a very readable novel on the subject. 'To Shed A Light' is a ficticious story based on fact of a funeral director - called Peter - who, dies suddenly

and has to watch his loved ones struggling with the trauma of his death, exacerbated by the fact that, although he spent his life helping other people cope with bereavement and knows how important it is to formulate plans ahead of time, he has not in fact made the proper preparations for his own demise.

In order to help people avoid the torment which the family undergoes, the company is happy to visit them at their own homes to discuss their wishes and 'shed a light' on the sensitive subject of death.

Pre-payment plans for funerals can also be set up, which again can eliminate much of the anxiety surrounding funeral arrangements. The company's flexible approach will ensure that all arrangements are made in accordance with the wishes of those concerned while observing the appropriate financial constraints. Economies can, for instance, be effected by judicious use of modern materials; veneered chipboard can be substituted for solid oak to produce a more economic but entirely suitable coffin which will in no way detract from the dignity of the occasion.

As the company approaches its 125th anniversary, it is very proud of its history as a family business and of its long association with the community it serves. The glossy black Belgian horses and the glass-sided hearses which conveyed Tom Junior's contemporaries to their places of rest have been replaced by a fleet of modern purpose-built vehicles, but local families who have used the services of Neville Funeral Service for many generations continue to enjoy the same high level of service. The company itself has been in the stewardship of five generations of the Neville and Henman families, and the firm continues to build on the wealth of experience and expertise which has accumulated over this time to provide the best possible service to the community of the Shires.

Below: The Company premises on Marsh Road, Leagrave. **Bottom:** *The fleet outside the Police Station in the 1950s.*

The two local families that went from nursery to haulage depot

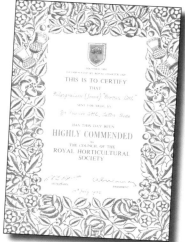

Francis Little first became interested in market gardening when, as a soldier in the Wiltshire Regiment, he came to Luton on demob leave in 1919 to visit his Uncle Jesse. During the war the young man had been taken prisoner of war and placed on a farm, where he had worked hard and been well looked after in return. Now he made himself so useful at his uncle's nursery in North Luton that Jesse offered him a job there, and taught him the secret of growing cucumbers, tomatoes and chrysanthemums.

Within a few years Francis had become Nursery Foreman and was happily settled in Luton with his wife Maud whom he married in 1921 and their two children: son Aubrey, born in 1922, and daughter Daphne, born in 1924. They had also made some good friends, including solicitor John Gates. Francis and Maud wanted to own their own business one day. Francis put aside the money he got by selling cabbage, Brussells plants and celery grown on his own little patch of land; meanwhile he worked hard at his uncle's nursery, and

Maud, who was a professional dressmaker and costumier, made clothes for the local ladies and earned herself a good reputation.

By 1929 the couple's savings were healthy. Francis' brother had moved out to Australia to make a fresh start, and the idea of joining him was tempting, but on the advice of John Gates they went to look at a piece of land which was for sale at Tythe Farm, Toddington Road. A house was being built on the adjoining site, and with John's help they were able to buy both house and land, and then proceed to establish their nursery. Francis built the propagating greenhouse first, and, having sowed seeds, started work on four more greenhouses while his seeds germinated. Their first cucumbers were ready early in 1930, and once the nursery began to bring in a steady income, Maud gave up her dressmaking to help Francis in the nursery. During that first year Francis built

*Above left: Arthur Meeks, the founder of Meeks Transport. **Above right:** A certificate awarded to the company by the Royal Horticultural Society for one of its creations **Below:** The Little Nursery in the 1950s.*

another quarter acre of greenhouses, and the future looked bright for the family; but the following October Maud died suddenly during a bad 'flu epidemic, leaving Francis devastated, with a seven-year-old and a nine-year-old to look after and a business to run.

Throughout the difficult period that followed, he was supported by John Gates, who had regularly spent his Sundays with the family; fifteen-year-old employee Robert Currington, too, rendered invaluable assistance. Robert was to stay with the firm for 50 years, and continued to work part-time even after his retirement. So the business kept going, and over the years Francis built it up, running

Above left: Francis Little relaxing iwth the family and his 'beloved Oldsmobile'. Above right: Aubrey Little in his RAF days. Top: Francis Little with Beatrice Dale in the tomato packing shed in a picture from the 1960s.

to 44 greenhouses, including eight very large houses especially for tomatoes. He also built two packing sheds, where cucumbers and tomatoes destined for London's Covent Garden Market were sorted, packed and loaded onto lorries several times a week. In addition Francis began to grow chrysanthemums and geraniums.

Meanwhile, various local ladies had come in to cook and look after the house when their own family commitments permitted, but inevitably the time came when none of the neighbours was in a position to take on extra work. The problem was solved when his cousin Miss Beatrice Dale agreed to come and help out until he found someone else; and the arrangement worked so well that it became permanent. Beatrice was a florist by trade, and enjoyed helping in the nursery when she had time. Francis named his special variety of geranium, a dwarf type with exceptionally large blooms, after her; 'Beatrix Little' was regularly shown at the Chelsea Flower Show, and became very popular.

Aubrey, too, had taken great pleasure in helping his father in the nursery as he grew up, so that by the time he left school in 1937 he had little left to learn. By 1939 the nursery had grown to four acres of glass on an eleven acre site. Then war broke out. Bob Currington went into the Army. Aubrey joined the Air Force. It became difficult to obtain fuel for heating the greenhouses. Recruiting labour was not a major problem, however; Francis must have been reminded of his own wartime experiences in the first war when he took on a group of German prisoners-of-war, and he also employed some older men and some local ladies who worked part-time; many of these stayed on long after the end of the war.

Aubrey and Bob returned to the business after the war, and in 1947 Aubrey's sister Daphne married and went to live in Tonbridge, where she and her husband Mac Court started a nursery. Their daughter Sally, Francis's first grandchild, was born in 1949. The following year Aubrey married Pat, and about the same time Francis and his cousin Beatrice launched a florist business. They kept a small flower shop for ten years or so, until Francis, who was nearing 70, decided it was time to start taking things a bit easier; but before he got round to retiring he died suddenly in 1964, at the age of 71.

The business was handed down to Aubrey. However, the 50s had proved a difficult decade; competition from Channel Islanders, and particularly from the Dutch, who benefited from government fuel subsidies while the price of coal in England kept rising. With this handicap British growers stood little chance, and when in 1968 Wimpeys made Aubrey an offer for five acres of land, a family meeting was held to discuss the future of the nursery. It was decided

Above right: *A Bedford lorry owned by the company in the 1950s.* ***Top:*** *a 'Walk and talk' held at Francis Little's premises in the 1950s.*

to take advantage of this opportunity to change direction. The five acres were sold to Wimpeys, further land was sold for development and four acres were kept. By the end of 1968 the family had become owners of Meeks Transport.

Arthur Meeks, the founder of Meeks Transport, had been a friend of Francis Little. He was also a well-known figure locally, having become involved in politics in the latter part of his life; he was elected County Councillor in March 1946 and went on to become a County Alderman, and also held the post of Chairman of the Bedfordshire County Council Fire Brigade Committee. As a child he had lived first in Tavistock Street; his family had next moved to Baker Street where his Mother had opened a small shop, and then to Cambridge Street where they took over the corner shop. Arthur went to Surrey Street School and was for many years a member of Bailey Hill Methodist Chapel. He had a motorbike, and was interested in mechanical things, but like Francis he was also a keen nurseryman. He moved to Sherwood Road, then to Toddington Road, where Francis' uncle had once lived; there Arthur kept several greenhouses, using one of them to house orchids. He bought his first truck in 1933, a four-ton Bedford, and set up in business as a haulage contractor, doing a lot of work for the local railway companies and the Bedfordshire brickfields. By the time of his death in 1967, Meeks Transport had built up a name for reliability and good service and was running a large fleet of vehicles; so when it was put up for sale, Aubrey and Daphne Little saw it as a viable investment.

In 1970 the first warehouse was built and Meeks was moved to the former nursery site, where the two companies were run as separate operations; Francis Little & Son Limited was run by Aubrey and Daphne, while A E Meeks Ltd (Transport) retained many of its existing personnel. Long-standing employees who moved with the firm included managing director John Attenborough, traffic manager David Deller and workshop foreman John Blackmore, and the two latter are still with the company at the time of writing. When Meeks' former site was sold in 1973, the money raised was used to add another warehouse. Today, the former nursery site is a three-and-a-half acre haulage and warehousing depot, with a fleet of 14 vehicles ranging from 17 to 32 tonnes, 40,000 square feet of storage, and a fully-equipped workshop. The company has built up an extensive and loyal customer base and its reputation is firmly established.

With the Meeks family no longer represented, the Little family continues to run both businesses. Francis Little's third generation consists of Aubrey and Pat's twin sons Peter and Charles, and Daphne and Mac's daughter Sally and son Graham - born three months after his father tragically died of polio. At the time of writing Aubrey Little is in his late seventies and still works part-time; Peter, having served in the Royal Navy, joined Meeks Transport in 1978 and became managing director in 1986, while his brother Charles, a chartered accountant, keeps a watchful eye on the company's books.

The histories of both family businesses are characterised by hard work and employee loyalty; with many of their current employees boasting 25, 30 and 35 years' service, and managing director Peter Little still happy to drive when necessary, it is clear that these traditional values remain as strong as ever after 70 years, and will continue to bring the firm the success it deserves in the future.

Above: *A 25 years' service presentation to David Deller (centre) of a model lorry by Chairman Aubrey Little (right). Present MD Peter Little is on the left, wishing he had one!* ***Left:*** *John Attenborough's retirement in 1986. Peter Little (MD from 1986) is second from the left.* ***Below:*** *The company's premises today.*

The secret of their success lies in letting their skills go to waste . . .

When the company which was to become F & R Cawley Ltd was established in 1947 by Reg and Molly Cawley, the concept of waste management meant little to the founder or to anyone else - in those days waste material was just that, to be disposed of wherever was most convenient. R D Cawley, or Reg, as he was known, was a civil engineer, and an experienced one, having spent some years as General Manager of another local civil engineering business before starting his own business, which for the first five years or so traded as Stanbridges (Luton) Ltd,

before changing to its present style and title in 1952. It was around this time that Reg was joined by his brother Frank. Frank, like Reg, had gained experience of the civil engineering profession by working for another local firm, and when Reg and Frank joined forces their company was able to accept and carry out an increasing number of civil engineering and associated haulage contracts. Operating from the small site in Wingate Road which was the company's first home - and which is still owned by them today - their principal activity throughout the 50s and early 60s was road building, although they also undertook earth moving and transportation for the sand and ballast industry. During these early years the company was engaged on the building of the A6 Clophill by-pass, and was a major supplier of road building materials to the M1 construction project - the M1, of course, was the country's very first motorway.

Left: RD Cawley, the company's founder.
Below: Molly Cawley (née Ferry) together with her parents outside The Royal Oak in Leagrave which they ran for many years.

Other major projects during this era included bulk excavation for the Vauxhall Spare Parts Factory and material supply to the test track at Millbrook. The company's fleet of small tippers was also used to remove ashes and some factory waste from Laportes, Electrolux and George Kents; and this removal of waste which at first was seen as a supplementary use of the firm's resources was in fact by the late 60s the start of the waste disposal business. The company was one of the earliest users of the Dempster Dumpster waste collection system.

By this time Frank Cawley had left the company; Reg Cawley had bought his shares, and continued to run the company as sole proprietor from the late 60s until his death in 1972. In 1971 he was joined by his son Jonathan, who was principally engaged in helping run and expand the waste disposal business. After Reg's death Brian Cawley joined his brother Jonathan to take control of the earth moving and building material supply site.

During the 70s it was the waste disposal side of the business which proved to be the growth area; but while it continued to flourish and expand, the bulk earth moving and material supply side slowly contracted, although it was still involved with major projects in Milton Keynes such as the construction of the new Coca Cola factory and the new sewerage works being built at East Hyde. By the end of the 70s the company was operating 40 vehicles and associated plant and equipment.

With more and more waste materials passing through its hands, the company realised that much of the material which had traditionally been destined for landfill was in fact capable of being re-used, and that it would in fact be in everybody's interests to do so. As a result of this line of thinking, two significant developments came about at the beginning of the 80s. The first was that the company built a Waste Reclamation Factory on its existing site, aimed at minimising the amount of waste taken to landfill. One of the first of its kind in the country, this was followed by a scaled-down version at one of the main contracts at the time, New Covent Garden Fruit and

Above left: One of the Company's first tippers.
Top: Transport Manager George Mapp.

Vegetable Market in Nine Elms, South London. Secondly, the firm bought a new transport depot near to the existing one to help accommodate the company's rapid expansion.

By the end of the 80s the company was well established in the waste management and recycling industry, and found themselves at the forefront of the movement towards recycling as public interest was aroused and environmental lobbying gained momentum. Bulk earth moving activities and material supply were curtailed as Jon and Brian decided to focus on waste collection. Rapid expansion followed as they became involved in glass recycling and bulk haulage of recycled materials. The company also took over several smaller skip hire and waste disposal companies during the 80s, and the increase in business culminated in an additional depot and Waste Transfer Station in Milton Keynes.

The next step was to invest in a wider range of specialised equipment to enable the company to offer the complete range of waste management services and become a 'one stop shop'. A Liquid Tanker division was started up, and this now comprises six vehicles specialising in the collection and treatment of all types of liquid wastes. Known as Cawley Tankers, the operating depot is situated on an adjoining site purchased by the company at about the same time. This site also houses the firm's workshops and maintenance facilities.

Despite the recession of the early 90s the company continued to invest in the latest waste collection plant and equipment. In 1997, work was completed on a new 40,000 square foot Materials Recycling Factory incorporating new offices and a concreted transport depot, representing an investment of some £2 million. This carefully-designed facility ensures not only a streamlined and highly efficient operation, but also a clean and comfortable working environment for the operatives. Because of the infinite variety of materials coming in, much of the work can only be done manually. At any one time up to 30 operatives can be working at the picking stations, sorting and baling metal, wood, cardboard, paper and plastics for reprocessing. Operating from five sites in Wingate Road totalling some five acres,

Below: *Working on A6 Bypass.* **Bottom:** *Stan Coles, George Smith and colleague taking a break.*

liquids. Many offices in and around Luton recycle their scrap paper through Cawley's Office Paper Recycling Scheme and consign their confidential documents to F & R Cawley for destruction - while the bottles left over from the office party can be disposed of discreetly at one of the firm's many bottle banks throughout the region!

As more and more organisations opt to dispose of their waste in an environmentally responsible way, F & R Cawley is happy to work with them, to advise and assist in deciding upon an environmental strategy to meet their particular needs, to put the necessary systems into place, and even to carry out audits on the amount of waste disposed of. At the University of Hertfordshire's campus,

the company is now able to provide a completely integrated waste management and recycling service to its customers. A depot has recently been opened in Wellingborough and it is planned to invest in improved recycling facilities at Milton Keynes.

Half a century after its foundation, F & R Cawley is now established throughout Bedfordshire, Buckinghamshre, Hertfordshire and Nottinghamshire as a leader in the field of waste management. Large manufacturers such as Vauxhall, IBC Vehicles, Mercedes and T & E Neville rely on Cawley to collect their waste products, as do Luton Airport, the University of Hertfordshire, and most of the Tesco stores in the region. The company handles several thousands of tonnes of waste material per week, much of it packaging waste such as card, plastic and polythene, but also metal, wood and

for instance, F & R Cawley's waste collection service includes multiple kerbside collection points around the 2,000 student residences, while some manufacturers need to be sure that there will be no unauthorised access to discarded items. Customers are invariably impressed by the personal service which they receive from F & R Cawley, backed by attention to detail, so that whatever the organisation's requirements they can rely on Cawley's expertise, experience and equipment to provide the most efficient waste management solution.

*Above: Left to right back; Frank Morriss, Will Macgonigle and Brian Thomas. Front; Jonathan Cawley, Molly Cawley and Brian Cawley with local MP Kelvin Hopkins in the vehicle. **Top**: Brian Cawley with Keith Hart and Dave Watson (centre) together with a group of employees.*

Who says the earth isn't flat?

Constructing a new factory, supermarket or housing estate is tremendous undertaking. To the man - or woman - in the street, the process of building seems to consist of a period of completely random activity by a hoard of busy men in hard hats and reflective clothes, driving noisy dirty machines, and then suddenly, as if by magic, a recognisable building appears in the middle of it all and begins to grow of its own accord. In fact, of course, all that seemingly random activity conceals a great deal of skill, and one of the very first steps is to make sure that the site is flat to begin with. Floors need to be level. Just imagine living in a house where your furniture kept sliding towards the back door, or shopping in a supermarket where you had to push your trolley up a steep incline to get to the bread, and hang on to it to stop it running away while you stopped picked your vegetables. Over the last 50 years Luton has seen many such

Above: *Fred Thomas, founder of the company.*
Below: *A driver, Ozzie Peach in a Thames Trader tipper lorry c1958 at Upper George Street, Luton.*

buildings grow out of nothing: housing estates at Runfold Avenue, Farley Hill, Marsh Farm and Wigmore; factories on Sundon Park, Capability Green, Cosgrave Way and many more industrial estates; and the Arndale Centre, built between 1969 and 1974. All these buildings have nice flat floors, and the company which made sure of it is Thomas Bros (Luton) Limited.

Thomas Bros began in 1947 as a private partnership between brothers Fred and George Thomas. The Thomas family had moved to Luton in the early 1930s, just before Fred reached his teens; they had lived for a while in Dagnell before that, but came originally from Flamstead, where they had been farmers. They settled in well in Luton; the family attended church at St Luke's, Leagrave where Fred Thomas was in the choir and became an altar server at the age of 12, continuing until he was 73! Mr Thomas senior worked with horses and carts and undertook road work, employing Irish labour with his two older sons. When Fred was 17, his father bought him a tipper lorry and employed a man to teach him to drive, and his brother George followed in his footsteps. The lorry replaced some of the horses and carts. At the age of 20 Fred married Frankie whom he had met at St Luke's - they later had three sons, Greg, Howard and Paul.

In 1940 Fred volunteered for the RAF where he was to remain until he was demobbed in late 1946. During the war both Fred and George, who had also joined the RAF, served abroad as aircraft fitters, mostly in the Middle East. When they returned to

civilian life - Fred having risen to the rank of
Sergeant - they decided to go into business together.
Their father had bought a house and yard in Nursery
Road, Leagrave in 1939, and this was where, in 1947,
the brothers set up their business. To begin with
their main activity was carting surplus excavated
material from construction sites to spoil tips, now
known as landfill sites. The work was very labour-
intensive as the lorries were to a very large extent
loaded by hand. George mostly took care of vehicle
maintenance while Fred dealt with customers, and
they were assisted by Fred's wife Frankie who acted
as secretary, looking after the accounts, answering
the telephone and liaising between George and Fred
and their clients.

Above: *Excavating for and lowering new petrol tanks
in Manyweathers Garage, in London Road, Luton in
the early 1960s.*

Nineteen fifty saw Thomas Bros breaking new ground,
as it were, purchasing a new mechanical loading shovel
which was a completely new innovation for the
construction industry and revolutionised the time taken
to load lorries. The 50s were a very busy time for the
company, as the post-war building programme involved
the development of many new housing sites and new
road links. The tireless hard work of the founders,
combined with their forward-thinking approach and
readiness to invest in new equipment, kept Thomas
Bros ahead of the competition, and the company
continued to prosper and grow; at its largest, the
Thomas fleet comprised some 25 lorries. Customers,
then as now, were mainly builders and civil engineers
engaged on construction contracts within a 40 mile
radius of Luton.

The building industry continued to thrive into the 1960s
with major projects such as construction at Luton

Airport, where Thomas Bros was involved in the Britannia hangar development. In 1972 the decision was made to convert to a limited company, and Thomas Bros (Luton) Ltd was formed with Greg Thomas, Fred's son, as Managing Director.

Unfortunately for Greg, recession began to affect all aspects of industry in the mid 70s, shortly after he assumed overall responsibility for running the business, and it was extremely difficult for the company to find sufficient work at rates which reflected true costs. However, thanks to the firm's policy of investing heavily during the boom years, its survival was never in question and its workforce's jobs were secure; no employee was made redundant either during this recession or during the recession of the 90s. Work continued on Luton's Arndale Centre Development until 1974, and the firm was also involved in major road construction projects around this time. Work began in the mid 70s on the section of Luton Inner Ring Road between Castle Street and Crawley Green Road, and in 1977 improvements to the A6 at Barton Cutting meant that Thomas

Above: A Smith 12 and Thames Trader in Upper George Street/Stuart Street at the new Royal Insurance offices in the early 1960s.
Right: *A Commer 2 stroke in the 1950s.*

Bros Ltd was called upon to remove of some 100,000 tons, or 60,000 cubic metres, of chalk. This project was to widen the existing road, provide a crawler lane for lorries and create a dual carriageway in part of the cutting, and in order to effect this it was necessary to flatten a chalk hill. The material was removed to the valley on the other side of the road, and the operation took some five months, with 100 lorry-loads of chalk being shifted every day.

Earth-moving equipment has become many times larger and more reliable over the 50 years that Thomas Bros has been in the business, although mechanical excavators and tipper lorries still form the basic tools of the trade. The company has invested heavily in new plant and equipment, and now has a mixed fleet of Caterpillar excavators, bulldozers and loading shovels, its own low loader to transport its equipment, and a fleet comprising fifteen 32 tonne tipper lorries. All equipment is maintained it the company's own workshops. The company still operates from its original premises in Nursery Road, although the original house has now been demolished.

Bulk excavation remains the core service offered today, with the company specialising in earthwork construction projects and site

decontamination. Various other ancillary services are also provided, namely demolition, plant hire, landfill and site clearance works; Thomas Bros was responsible for the restoration of the Luton Airport refuse tip to recreational use, and for various open spaces for Luton Parks Department, within Luton Borough Council. Other projects in recent years have included further work at Luton Airport, including the raising of the runway on the north eastern end in 1988, the new Monarch hangar in the early 90s and many other sites developed as part of the airport's expansion; one very recent project for which excavation work was completed in March 1999 is the new Luton Airport Parkway Station. Vauxhall Motors has also become a regular client; one of the largest projects which Thomas Bros has undertaken for them was the massive new Paint Shop, built in 1985. Thomas Bros is in fact the only specialist earthmoving contractor based in Luton, and its lorries and excavators have been involved in literally hundreds of building sites as Luton has expanded in the last 50 years.

In 1997 Thomas Bros (Luton) Ltd celebrated its 50th anniversary; many of its employees joined the founding family in looking back over this period, as the company is proud of its long-serving workforce, and the workers appreciate the benefits of working for a family-run firm which values each individual employee and which has always done its best to ensure job security for them, even in times of recession. Sadly, two years after the firm's 50th anniversary its founder and Chairman Fred Thomas died, on 23rd February 1999, at the age of 79.

The company has survived the difficult times, and now, with a favourable economic climate and the outlook for the building industry looking very promising, Thomas Bros is confident of the future. Greg Thomas has a young, dynamic management team consisting of estimator, contracts manager and surveyor, and a committed workforce who will continue to maintain Thomas Bros' high-profile presence on the streets of Luton. The company is aware that the size of its lorries means that it is not always popular with the motoring public. Just occasionally the smart green lorries, with the familiar red stripe on the front, have been known to deposit mud on the road, adjacent to building sites in wet weather conditions. The company would therefore like to take this opportunity of apologising, and promises it will try not to do this again. It would, however, like to point out that factories, shops and supermarkets like their floors to be level, and considerable excavation work is needed to achieve this, especially in the hilly areas of Luton. The world was not, in fact, created flat; the only way to make it so, is to bring in green and red lorries of Thomas Bros (Luton) Ltd.

Left: *Excavation work undertaken in March 1994.* **Below:** *One of the company's present fleet.*

The Luton company that sets its sights on success through success on its sites

Many readers will remember the demolition of properties in Church Street in 1968 to make way for the town's revolutionary new shopping centre. The many compulsory purchase orders served at that time came as a shock to a number of firms; and among them was the Luton Building Company, who discovered that the premises which they had occupied for 45 years were to be demolished.

Frank Chown, Jack Buckingham and Arthur Smith had purchased the cottage in Church Street in 1923, when they first formed Luton Building Company. By May 1925 the company was sufficiently well-established to take on additional administrative staff, who may well have assisted with a rather tricky problem which arose that year. As part of a contract for the Borough of Luton, the company was supposed to move the Ames Memorial, an ornate drinking fountain known locally as the 'Pepper Pot'. The memorial stood on Market Hill, where it had been first erected, and the plan was to relocate it at a new site in Manor Road. Unfortunately, moving it proved to be out of the question, as it was in too bad a state to survive the transfer. The decision was taken to scrap it, and its remains were duly dropped down a disused well in Luton Building Company's yard in Church Street; scrupulous as ever, the company thereupon repaid £25.0s.0d to the Borough of Luton in respect of the work they had been unable to carry out. Visitors to the Arndale Centre today might care to spare a thought for the remains of the 'Pepper Pot', incarcerated at the bottom of a filled-in well, deep below their feet.

As the country's economy recovered from the effects of the first world war Luton Building Company prospered, soon expanding into the adjoining cottages and land in Church Street. Early changes in personnel included founder Arthur Smith leaving and Hector Groom and Fred Sawyer joining; the latter was appointed Office Boy, a position which has proved, over the years, to offer very good prospects. Another of the founders, Jack Buckingham, died unexpectedly in 1932. This left Frank Chown in

Above: *Frank Chown, one of the founders.*
Below: *Company offices in Church Street until April 1969.*

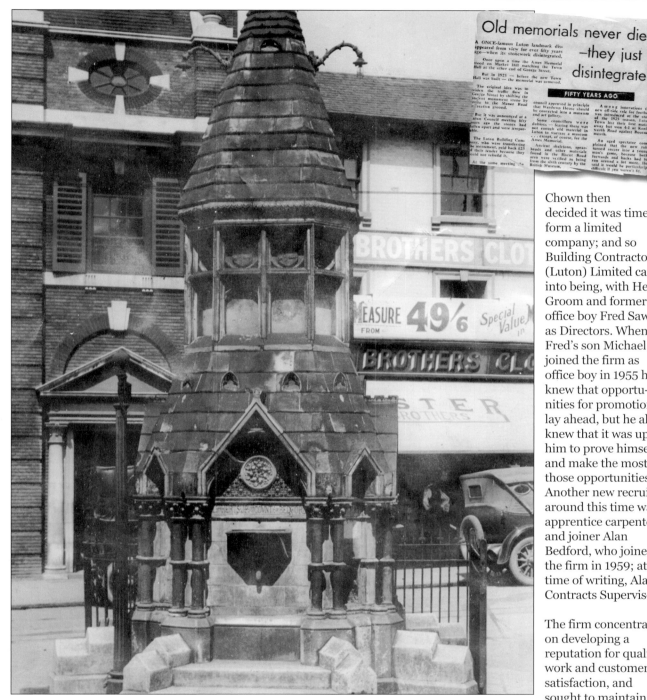

Chown then decided it was time to form a limited company; and so Building Contractors (Luton) Limited came into being, with Hector Groom and former office boy Fred Sawyer as Directors. When Fred's son Michael joined the firm as office boy in 1955 he knew that opportunities for promotion lay ahead, but he also knew that it was up to him to prove himself and make the most of those opportunities. Another new recruit around this time was apprentice carpenter and joiner Alan Bedford, who joined the firm in 1959; at the time of writing, Alan is Contracts Supervisor.

The firm concentrated on developing a reputation for quality work and customer satisfaction, and sought to maintain this

charge of the growing company. The building boom continued until the second world war, and the company continued to thrive; and when war arrived it was kept busy with the war effort, constructing the Vauxhall Motors factory where the Churchill Tank was built, and also the first phase of the Bedford Truck factory at Dunstable.

In 1946, with peace restored, the firm acquired some land in Ridgway Road which it used for storage. Frank

through the diverse range of activities which developed over the next decade, working seven days a week when necessary to ensure timely completion. Contracts ranged from new build to alterations and maintenance work, with new construction projects including a branch library, a coach station and a banana warehouse, and the company also undertook day to day factory maintenance.

Frank Chown, the remaining founder, died in 1963, leaving the company in the hands of Fred Sawyer and Hector Groom, and the name reverted to Luton Building Company Limited. When Luton's redevelopment plans were announced in 1968, Fred, assisted by Michael who

Top left: *The 'Pepperpot', dismantled by the company in 1925.* ***Left:*** *Fred Sawyer - who started working for the company as office boy in 1925 and retired in 1995.*

true to form had long since moved on from being office boy, entered into protracted negotiations with the local Planning Department to identify a suitable alternative location, while at the same time doing their best to keep the business running smoothly. Eventually permission was obtained to build new offices and a joinery workshop on land which they were using as storage in Ridgway Road. Before this was completed, however, Hector Groom retired. Michael Sawyer joined his father on the board, and in April 1969 they organised the move into their purpose-built premises in Ridgway Road, effectively putting a stop to the rumours which had begun to circulate amongst sceptics that the company was to cease trading. Fred and Michael, supported by a loyal workforce and an equally loyal clientele, worked hard to minimise the disruption caused by the move, and by the time the company reached its 50th anniversary in 1973 it was well established at Ridgway Road, with a great deal to celebrate.

Business was good during the years which followed, with the company carrying out major contracts for both new and existing clients. Among the many clients with whom Luton Building Company has been regularly

> *By the time the company reached its 50th birthday in 1973 it was well established in Luton and the surrounding areas*

associated over the years are the University of Luton, London Luton Airport, Vauxhall, Electrolux, Sainsbury, Halfords, Legal and General, the Chamber of Commerce, various local authorities and the Ancient Monuments division of the Ministry of Works. Some of these associations are very long-standing indeed; Vauxhall Motors has been a customer since 1925, and the company has done such a wide range of work for them that, as Michael Sawyer says, 'About the only thing we have not done for Vauxhall is build a car.' The work which the company has done for the Ancient Monuments division has been particularly diverse and challenging, calling for unusual skills and special materials which have to be sourced from around the country.

During the 1980s two more likely lads were recruited as office boys: Trevor Sawyer and Adrian Sawyer, Michael's sons. Doreen Gray, who is currently Secretary and Personal Assistant, joined in 1989, and by that time the recession was beginning to have an impact on virtually every sector of industry. Luton Building Company rose

Above: *Showroom built by the company for Vauxhall Motors Ltd in the 1930s, which they have also recently refurbished.*

to the challenge; with its loyal client base, its dedicated workforce and its experienced management team, it was in a strong position, and pulled through the recession with no loss of jobs.

Sadly, in October 1995 Fred Sawyer died, just a few months after retiring from the company which had been part of his life for 70 years, and which he had guided through the difficult years and built up into the well-respected firm that it is today.

Fred's grandsons Trevor and Adrian became company directors in April 1997. The management of the company today consists of Michael Sawyer as managing director and chairman, and Trevor and Adrian as directors; Trevor is responsible for procuring work, and Adrian for liaising with clients during the works and ensuring a successful conclusion.

In 1998 the firm celebrated 75 successful years by holding a Dinner Dance at the Chiltern Hotel in Luton. More than a hundred guests were present at the occasion to pay tribute to the company which has always placed people high on its list of priorities. Customer satisfaction has always been one of Luton Building Company's prime concerns, and it was gratifying that so many clients showed their appreciation by joining in the celebrations at the Chiltern Hotel. The large numbers of employees and ex-employees who were there too are a reflection of the close relationship between company and workforce; a large proportion of both staff and site personnel have been with the company for many years, often directly from school, and often following in the footsteps of other members of their family. Carpenters, joiners, groundworkers,

bricklayers, plasterers, decorators and other site workers are employed directly by the company. Luton Building Company has created a strong culture of loyalty and mutual support which has assured it of continued success during its first 75 years, and as it embarks on fourth quarter of its first century it remains as committed as ever to serving the interests of both its clients and the many people who rely on it for a living.

Left: *From left to right: Adrian, Michael and Trevor Sawyer.*
Below: *A pair of houses built in 1938. These were the first houses in Fairford Avenue.*

The dyeing craft that still caps them all

It is Baxter Hart & Abraham's proud claim that they have been dyeing for a living for almost 150 years. Today they are successful commission dyers, dyeing hat materials for millinery manufacturers and a variety of other fabrics for use in industry all over the world. The company's origins can be traced back, on the one side, to the dyeworks at 36/38 Wellington Street, Luton, run by Mr George Abraham in 1864 and passed down first to son John, then in 1894 to grandson Henry; and on the other side, to the partnership formed between Mr Baxter Herbert Hart and Mr Edward Burgess in 1904. Trading as Baxter Hart & Company, with Mr Burgess in charge of sales and accounts and Mr Hart acting as both bleacher and works manager, this firm's business consisted of bleaching straw plaits for the hatmaking industry.

In the 19th and early 20th century nearly all hats for both men and women were made from straw. Bedfordshire's chalky soil was found to produce the best quality straw and reeds for hatmaking, and so Britain's hat industry grew up in this area and formed the basis of Luton's economic development throughout the 19th century. Straw plaiting had been a cottage industry in Great Britain for many centuries, not only in the Bedfordshire area but also to some extent in Devon, Essex, Suffolk, Yorkshire and the Orkneys, and provided many people with a good living during the 19th century; straw would be obtained locally, the plaiting was often done by

women and children, and trading was carried out at plait markets where plait traders would buy from the families who made them and sell to hat manufacturers. However, around 1870 the local craftsfolk found themselves having to compete with imported plaits from China which could be obtained very cheaply; although the quality of the Cantonese straw was arguably inferior, the material was nonetheless perfectly suitable for hatmaking, and so the prices of plaits fell dramatically, to the extent that most families found that plaiting was no longer profitable. Soon very few local plaiters remained.

So the straw plaits which Baxter Hart & Company bleached were imported from China, and at that time their main use was in the manufacture of straw boater-

*Top left : Henry Abraham c1908. **Above left:** Aubrey C Horn - 1920. **Above right:** Charles E and Catherine (nee Abraham) Horn. **Below:** A family stall at Luton Plait Market.*

style hats, or Boaters, which it was the fashion for gentlemen to wear during the summer months. Then, in the 1920s, the firm diversified into dyeing the same kind of plaits for use on ladies' hats. In subsequent years the bleaching trade began to go into decline and the demand for dyeing increased rapidly, so that this became the main focus of their activities.

Mr Hart's son Clifford was brought into the firm to be trained as a dyer, and in 1925 Mr S B J Snoxell joined the firm, to take the place of Mr Burgess who was due to retire the following year. The firm was still involved in both the bleaching and dyeing of plaits, with a very large proportion of their bleaching work now being exported, mainly to South America. With the hat industry always keen to experiment with new styles and materials, in 1928 the firm began dyeing and finishing ribbons for use in trimming ladies' and gentlemen's hats.

In 1938 Baxter Hart & Company amalgamated with George Carruthers Limited, and expanded their business of dyeing plaits and hoods; the hood is the cone shape of a felt or straw hat. After the second world war and the years which followed, all materials were in very short supply; parachute silk was dyed into lingerie colours, and when nylon replaced pure silk in parachute fabrication, then nylon was dyed instead. In 1956 a further amalgamation took place, between Baxter Hart & George Carruthers Limited and H Abraham (Dyers) Limited. This firm had become a limited liability company some three years earlier, with Aubrey Charles Horn as Managing Director and his son Tony Charles Horn as a Director; the Horn family's connections in plait dealing

extend back to the 18th century, and Aubrey had acquired the business from Henry Abraham in 1933. Abraham's dyeworks had moved from its original site in Wellington Street to Charles Street and the corner of High Town Road, and the firm had set up its head office at 5 Barbers Lane. A felt hood factory was subsequently established at 50/52 York Street. At the time of the merger the directors of the newly-formed Baxter Hart & Abraham were B C Hart, A C Horn, T C Horn, S B J Snoxell and J S Snoxell.

The bleaching and dyeing trade was undergoing a period of contraction around this time, mainly because of the new synthetic fabrics which were becoming available and the variety of different materials being used in the manufacture of ladies' hats. Many of the smaller companies either closed or merged with other firms, and within the space of a few years the number of bleachers and dyers decreased from nearly 30 to a mere half dozen. Baxter Hart & Abraham, with a reduced number of employees, began to concentrate on supplying wool felt hoods and dyed ribbons to the millinery trade.

One of the companies with whom Baxter Hart & Abraham Limited formed a business association during the 1950s was Barford Brothers Limited of North Street. Barford Brothers is one of Luton's oldest-established dyers, having operated from the same premises in North Street since the firm was first started in 1894 by brothers Gilbert and Ernest Barford. The business was then handed down to Gilbert's sons Rex and Lance.

Above: Employees who worked with Henry Abraham before A C Horn (centre front) took over

After the end of the second world war it had set up production lines to make felt hoods, and also dyed petersham ribbon for hat decoration. In 1955 they became part of the Hubbard Group - Hubbards had started to produce felt hoods in 1919 - and shortly afterwards Rex and Lance, who continued to run the business, invested in a Bates Nylon Setting Machine; one of their earliest recorded business transactions with Baxter Hart & Abraham relates to the carrying out of ribbon setting processing on this machine. The company was bought back during the 60s and then sold to employees George Ostler and Michael Dellar. In the late 70s Barford Brothers, which at that time styled itself wool felt hood makers, bleachers and dyers, and galloon and Petersham dyers, amalgamated with Baxter Hart & Abraham Limited. Mr Dellar remained a director and was joined by T C Horn and J H Horn, and all dyeing operations were moved to North Street, while the merchanting was retained at 141 New Bedford Road.

During the mid 1980s another firm of dyers, Oakley Dyers in Grove Road, went into liquidation and was purchased by Barford Brothers Limited. This firm now trades as Grove Dyers Limited with R C Horn ACA and J H Horn as Directors.

Right: *Henry and Blanche Abraham on their 60th Wedding Anniversary during the 1940s.* **Below:** *A stand of the London and Luton Bleachers and Dyers Association at the British Industries Fair in London.*

The level of mechanisation used in dyeing has increased significantly over the years, with the development of machines which can dye ribbon and other materials in larger quantities and more evenly, but the old craft traditions remain important; although matching lamps now help to match colours, there is still no substitute for the human eye and an experienced judgement. Each dyeworks has its own 'trade secrets', and often, as is the case at Barfords, a dyeworks will design and produce its own machines to carry out its own exclusive processes.

and trimming - there was always a backlog of hoods waiting to go into the drying room, which prevented the dyeing and stiffening lines from running at full capacity. Once the heat pump dehumidifier and associated equipment had been installed, with a microprocessor to monitor temperature and humidity conditions in the room and maintain optimum air conditions, the humidity level dropped to between 20 and 30 percent. Under these conditions the hoods dried much faster and it became possible to dry two batches in a day, which meant that the dyeing and stiffening lines no longer had to stop production while the drying process caught up.

As Baxter Hart & Abraham and its subsidiary companies wait for another century to turn, they can look back on many changes. The cottage industry and the small family firms of the late 18th century have evolved into 20th century factories financed by major business investment. The 19th century straw plait merchant now deals in wool, fur hoods, petersham ribbon, veiling, flowers, feathers, hatpins, buckram and stiffeners as well as sisal and straw hoods. Some of the materials handled now had not been invented a hundred years ago. Services are no longer restricted to milliners; while the millinery trade itself has adopted a new progressive outlook. But essentially it is still a trade based on traditional crafts, a trade built around the values of the family business, and most of all a trade which is proud of its history.

The millinery trade today still uses traditional processes, although from time to time an opportunity arises to alter a process or introduce new machinery to improve efficiency or enhance the working environment. One such innovation at Barford Brothers was the introduction of a heat pump dehumidifier into the drying room in September 1992. Until then, hoods had been dried by floor-mounted steam coils which raised the temperature in the room. The problem with this system was that it created so much humidity that air in the room soon reached saturation point, and this slowed down the drying process. Only one room full of hoods could be dried in a day, and as each hood had to be dried twice during manufacture, once after dyeing and once after stiffening - the processes of hat manufacture being dyeing, drying, stiffening and drying again before shaping

*Top: Reg Costin and Frank Cooper collecting hoods which had been bleached and dried in sunlight at Baxter, Hart & Co in 1948. **Above left:** T C Horn being presented with a silver salver by Frederick Fox, at the end of his chairmanship of the Millinery Trades Benevolent Association in 1986.*

Accommodating people who are at home with quality

W hen young Michael Connolly arrived in Luton from his native Aughamore in Co. Mayo, Ireland back in 1958 with only the possessions he carried, little could he have dreamed of the major company he would build and the national house-building awards he would one day win.

"We got off the train at Kings Cross Station with only what we could carry," he recalled. "But that was the story of our generation."

Michael, who was born in County Mayo, was trained as a joiner and, abandoning earlier plans to be a woodwork teacher, came to England and started doing small jobs for the then Luton Corporation.

He worked and saved hard and in 1963 was able to buy his first, small site - at Harlington - with the help of a friendly bank manager from what was then the Westminster Bank.

Bank managers were very different in those days, Michael remembered. "He'd get on his bike and

Left: Michael Connolly, the founder of Connolly Homes. Below: The first Connolly bungalows built in Harlington.

afford to have anyone to answer the phone," said Michael. "Back in those days there was no such thing as a show house and there were very few new houses advertised."

That first advertisement worked well and the Connolly brothers received a stack of replies and soon sold those three pairs of semis.

Next came Abbey Close, a 21-plot site in Ampthill, followed by a third site in nearby Clophill where the Connolly brothers built more than 70 homes.

The business went from strength to strength, fulfilling Michael's 'game plan' at the time to double the number of legal completions each year.

come over to our site in Harlington for a cup of tea or see me in his back garden on a Saturday. He was a marvellous man."

Michael and his brothers, Bill and John, built six bungalows on that first site, doing all the work themselves and selling them for the princely sum of £2,050 each.

"We took out a small, run-on advert in the Luton News with a box number because we couldn't

And long gone are those early days when the young Michael Connolly would do not just the woodwork, but the plumbing and electrics, too!

Above: *Michael Connolly and wife Kathleen in 1960s.*
Top: *In the 1960s Ampthill Rural District Council handed over the 2,000th house it had completed since the war. Michael Connolly is in the centre.*

Above: Eric Morecambe was a guest at the opening of the Langford, Bedfordshire development opening in the late 1960s.
Below: Executive homes in Luton built in the 70s.

The thriving firm soon grew out of its 'greenhouse' office at the side of Michael's family home in Ashburnham Road, Luton, moving to proper offices in Cardiff Road and then, in 1969, to the present premises in Sarum Road.

The site included an old house, for which the tenant was paying the previous owners, the Co-op, £1 a week. The Connollys rehoused him in Stockingstone Road and kept his rent at just £1 a week until he died.

Today, the Sarum Road site - now known as Connolly House - is not only the group's head office but also houses a joiners' shop, plant department workshop and storage space.

By the end of the sixties, half of Connolly's business was private housing and the other half contract work for local authorities.

In 1968, John Connolly returned to his native Ireland where he set up a new Connolly operation in Dublin. And in the early 1970s, the group started a company in Devon, initially at Totnes (until they encountered the holiday traffic!) and then at Ashburton, and a further building operation based at Holywood in County Down, Northern Ireland.

By then, the Connollys were building up to 1,000 houses a year between their three operations, in Luton, Ashburton and Ireland. In the mid Seventies, recession hit and many building companies of all sizes went under. But, with careful management and not a little hard work and worry, the Connolly Group weathered the storm.

"It was a tough time then and I had an ulcer chopped out to prove it," said Michael.

Even in those hard times, though, the firm was putting something back into the struggling building industry and the community. It launched its own apprenticeship scheme in 1975, which is still running today and doing its bit to tackle the skill shortages of the nineties.

"Some of the people who were with us in the early days 30 years ago are still with us," said Michael, Chairman and Managing Director of the Connolly Group and still living in a Connolly home in Old Bedford Road, Luton.

Today, Connolly Homes employs a workforce of more than 250 and builds around 350 houses a year across the Home Counties and in Northern Ireland, from two-bedroomed homes to exclusive five-bedroomed family houses, with prices ranging from about £65,000 up to nearly a quarter of a million. And they offer an impressive array of features such as Upvc double glazed windows, luxury fitted kitchens and a host of other features as standard.

"Our policy at Connolly Homes plc is to develop and provide a range of houses in various styles and sizes, which reflect our high standards and good reputation," said Michael. "All our homes demonstrate our attention to detail and dedication to using traditional building methods together with

the latest technology, offering a home that is both architecturally and environmentally pleasing."

The company is now the largest private house builder in Bedfordshire and has won a string of accolades, including the prestigious Daily Express Newspaper Housebuilder of the Year, Best Regional House Builder, Beds and Bucks, the Royal Institute of British Architects Regional Award for excellence in housing design and several NHBC Top 100 awards.

*Above: A street scene of Connolly homes in Caddington, Bedfordshire. **Above Right:** A Connolly home in Greenfield.*

At ease with technology

Huntleigh Healthcare's products today make a tremendous difference to the quality of medical care throughout the world. Patients in Holland, Belgium, France, Germany, Australia, Singapore, South Africa and the USA, where Huntleigh has 100 percent owned subsidiaries, as well as the rest of the world, can rest more easily thanks to hospital equipment supplied through Huntleigh's sales divisions, offices and distribution networks in those countries. Many elderly and disabled people are able to enjoy an enhanced quality of life thanks to appliances obtained from the same sources. The range of innovative ways in which the company has applied technology to solve medical problems is quite astonishing, and what is even more astonishing is that an organisation which has become of such major importance should have grown out of one man's interest.

Working as an engineer during the 1940s, Rolf Schild was involved in the design, development and production of a variety of medical instruments and monitoring devices including heart-lung machines. In 1956 he set up his own company, SE Laboratories, with his partner, Peter Epstein, a friend who was a mechanical engineer. This company gained widespread recognition for its work with transducers and ultraviolet recorders, and its projects included the development of multi-channel recorders and test bed instrumentation systems for major aircraft companies. Rolf's interest in medical applications never left him, however, and he would put his engineering skills to valuable use in his spare time at the Hammersmith Hospital, where he had friends. Meanwhile SE

Laboratories, following public flotation in 1963, merged with EMI in 1966, and Rolf Schild became a Director of EMI's Electronics Division as well as being Chairman of SE Laboratories. Rolf's interest in hospital equipment led to his involvement in the first EMI X-ray brain scanner. He left EMI in 1972 on a policy disagreement to concentrate on other interests. In 1969 he had already bought an interest in a start-up medical equipment operation, for which he adopted the ingenious name of Flowtron-Aire, a name devised by his wife to effectively identify Rolf's products with comfortable notion of 'floating on air'.

Below: *The factory in Bilton Way, 1978 - 1987.*
Bottom: *Offices in Bilton Way, 1978 - 1987.*

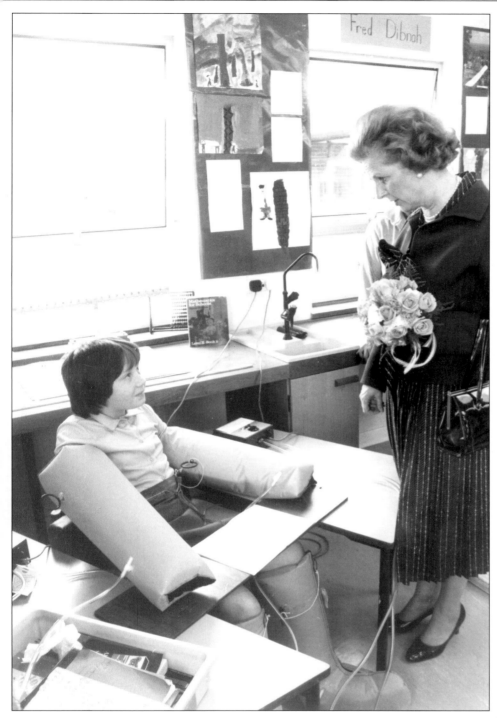

pooling and clotting. Controlled tests in 1973 at London hospitals including the Hammersmith showed a 90 per cent reduction in the incidence of DVT in high risk patients when the Flowtron-Aire device was applied to their legs before, during and after surgery. The concept was hailed as a great success; and it was discovered that varicose veins sufferers and those with rheumatism, leg ulcers and swelling also benefited from the device. The Flowtron Excel system for reducing the incidence of DVT continues to save lives today, and, in its modern form, with more sophisticated controls and with the plastic 'boots' replaced by a slimmer leg garment having a single air chamber, it remains an indispensable item of equipment in hospitals and nursing homes throughout the world.

At the time this device was launched, Flowtron-Aire was established at its first factory at 5a Lye Trading Estate, off the Old Bedford Road; it subsequently moved to Bilton Way. The chief output of these factories was support mattresses, which brought a modest profit, and in 1975 Flowtron-Aire was incorporated along with Rolf Schild's other business venture Micro Image Technology and Hymatic Engineering as the Huntleigh Group. The whole company was reorganised, with offices in Park Royal and factories in Redditch, and besides its medical involvement it had a strong interest in military equipment and the semi-conductor chemical industry. Business prospered and the group took the decision in 1983 to spin off the military division to concentrate on the design and manufacture of medical equipment, both for diagnosis and treatment. This company was floated on the USM market two years later.

One of Flowtron-Aire Limited's early devices was a non-invasive technique for reducing the incidence of thromboembolic disease, or deep vein thrombosis (DVT), which results principally from the pooling and clotting of blood in the legs when they are immobilised due to surgery, and which in 1971 claimed 257 lives per million head of population - almost as many victims as road traffic accidents, which in the same year killed 277 people per million head of population. The idea for the machine came from Dr J Pflug, a mountain rescue expert, and was an extension of the concept of the inflatable splint used in mountain rescue work. Dr Pflug brought his idea to Rolf Schild, who built a device which used an air pump to apply intermittent pressure through giant, air-filled, plastic 'boots' which encased the legs, and in this way the blood was prevented from

By this time Rolf's younger son David had joined him in the business. David's involvement had begun in 1984 when he had joined the company to learn the trade; he had spent some time on Research and Development before moving on to Production. Meanwhile Julian,

Rolf's older son, had studied modern history, graduating from Oxford University in 1981 and going on to gain experience with with Morgan Grenfeld and Coopers & Lybrand before joining his father's company as a fully qualified chartered accountant in 1987.

position of the individual patient, it has separate sections for the heels, thighs and legs, torso and head, and incorporates many features, including self-monitoring devices, a sophisticated alarm system, and a filtration system to reduce the risk of infection.

Nineteen eighty-seven brought further reorganisation with the closure of the offices in Park Royal and the purchase of a 45,000 sq. ft. factory and offices in Dallow Road. In 1993 the company acquired the adjoining Makita building in Finway. The purchase of an additional building of 15,000sq. ft. in Finway in 1997 brought the total factory and office space in Dallow Road to 120,000 sq. ft. Shortly after the removal of the entire operation to Luton, the company developed the concept for which it was to become world famous: the Nimbus® dynamic flotation system for patient support. This is a mattress which provides optimum pressure relief and comfort for patients - or, in layman's terms, helps stop long-term patients getting bed-sores. Automatically adjustable to the weight, size and

Today, Huntleigh Healthcare's range of products includes a tremendous number of devices and contraptions, some brilliantly simple and some amazingly complex, but all designed to improve the quality of life for those suffering from virtually any kind of infirmity. Besides those already mentioned, the company's products include hoists and lifters for those with limited mobility, physiotherapy and positioning equipment, plinths and couches for those suffering from sports injuries, stretchers and other ambulance and emergency equipment for accident victims, patient trolleys and

Top: *Jimmy Saville at the launch of Nimbus at Stoke Mandeville Hospital, 1989.*
Above: *An exterior view of Huntleigh Healthcare.*

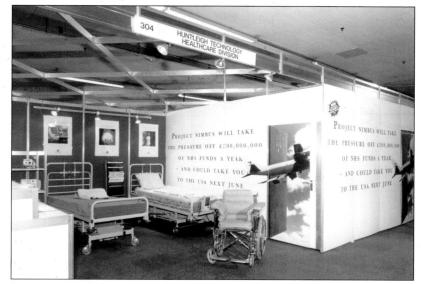

specialist hospital beds for in-patients, and a range of ultrasonic monitoring devices for vascular, obstetric and fetal monitoring. These products are manufactured at the Group's other UK sites at Wednesbury and Cardiff.

Such an impressive track record of innovative concepts and products can only be maintained by constant investment in research and development, and some 25 to 30 per cent of each year's profits are ploughed back into research and development. As well as its traditional hospital and nursing home clients, the company has in recent years found itself increasingly involved in supplying the homecare market both through Social Services and direct to private customers, reflecting the growing trend of caring for the elderly and disabled in their own homes wherever possible.

Huntleigh Healthcare is keenly aware of the importance of responding quickly to patient needs, and the organisation is geared to provide a rapid response delivery service. With 15 depots across the UK, it is able to access any hospital in the country within two hours of receiving an order for equipment. And because emergencies can happen at any hour of the day or night, its staff are on call 24 hours a day, seven days a week. On a day-to-day basis, regular contact is maintained with hospitals, and specialist staff can assist in budgeting by carrying out equipment audits and advising hospitals on the most efficient and cost-effective ways of meeting their equipment needs. Corporate growth

has continued in recent years, partly through acquisition and partly through product development and market expansion, and this will remain the trend for the foreseeable future. As Chairman of the company, Rolf Schild oversees the direction of the company and is in overall charge of the design of its products. Julian is currently Deputy Chairman and Group Finance Director, and David is Group Managing Director. An excellent team spirit exists within the organisation, which currently employs some 1,400 people worldwide, while its Luton-based workforce of around 550 makes it one of the largest employers in the area. It has a worldwide reputation for producing superior products which bring greater benefits in terms of medical effectiveness. Fittingly, the great achievements of both company and founder have not gone unrecognised; founder Rolf Schild has accumulated two Honorary Doctorates of Science - one from the University of Luton for personal inventions and innovations and the other from City University for his distinguished contribution to healthcare and medical instrumentation - the Royal Institute of Electrical Engineers' Achievement Medal, and an OBE for services to the medical industry; he has also recently been granted the Freedom of the City of London. The company has been awarded a succession of Queen's Awards for Export, and received the Queen's Award for Technology in 1993. And the gratitude of human beings the world over, who owe their recovery and their independence to Huntleigh's products, is immeasurable.

Top: Small exhibition stand at the Barbican in 1990 showing Nimbus. **Below:** *The largest UK stand, covering 4,000 sq. ft., at the Medica exhibition in Germany in 1998.*

The firm that drives all its customers away... in comfort and style!

In 1924, Alfred Seamarks left school and joined his father and older brother, Len, in their transport business at Higham Ferrers, Northants. His brother, Harry, joined the firm later. No doubt they hoped that their company would still be thriving 75 years later; but the idea of coach trips to destinations such as the

Granada TV studios, Paris' Disneyland, the Thames Barrier Exhibition Centre, leisure parks such as Alton Towers, the American Adventure Theme Park and Chessington World of Adventure, and shopping expeditions to the French hypermarkets would surely have left them gasping in amazement, back in 1937!

After the stage carriage service was sold to United Counties, the business moved to Rushden. Alfred and Harry, however, bought a business from Owen Smith in Westoning, Bedfordshire and they moved to the village on 10th April 1937.

The war years brought a variety of transport requirements which the company was able to meet. Its premises in Westoning became storage for up to three aircraft, with the wings removed. Coaches were seconded to the army, but later the firm was permitted to purchase more vehicles which it deployed on contracts to transport those engaged on aerodrome construction around Thurleigh. During the early 1940s, they bought the Luton business, Cosy Coaches of Oxen Road, High Town. With this company came a contract with Car Deliveries providing coaches to bring back drivers who had delivered lorries from Vauxhall to various M.O.D. depots.

In more recent years the company's wisdom in making Luton its home has become apparent. The development of Luton Airport gave Seamarks new opportunities for expansion. In the early days of Luton Airport in the late 1950s, Seamarks chartered Pegasus Airlines to Ireland and Jersey during the holiday season. In those days, there was no runway and the aircraft landed on grass. An airport office was set up, and express services between Luton Airport and Birmingham, Coventry, Leicester, Nottingham and London were run on behalf of the tour operator Skytours. Seamarks was also licensed to operate express services from central London to Luton Airport, which meant that it could carry passengers for any tour operator, and the opening of the M1 reduced the journey time to around an hour - with less time spent sitting in traffic than is often the case today!

Top right: *A line-up of Seamarks Coaches circa 1935.* ***Left:*** *The Bricklayers Arms Darts team on a day out to Yarmouth in June 1951.*

1955 was a landmark year when, during the rail strike, Seamarks' coaches delivered newspapers to various parts of the country for Fleet Deliveries of London. Following this, Seamarks was contracted to the Midland Bank to carry its staff to and from the London banks during rail strikes. This contract continued until the 1990s.

The 1960s saw Seamarks Bros Ltd established as the biggest independent licensed coach operator in Bedfordshire. Its smart cream-and-green coaches were a familiar sight on the county's roads, and passengers enjoyed all the latest luxuries, which at that time meant forced-air ventilation, interior heaters, radiomobile receivers and a public address system.

Another of Luton's success stories in recent years has been the growth of its University, and this again has provided opportunities for Seamarks. Today the firm is responsible for much of the University Student Union coach travel, taking Students' Union members to and from social outings, sporting activities and other expeditions throughout the year.

Other regular commitments include school runs, educational visits and corporate outings. Leisure day trips and shortbreak holiday tours are a very important part of its activities, and each year a varied programme is planned to offer local people a wide choice of affordable

excursions. As well as theme parks and family attractions, trips on offer include scenic and city tours and visits to stately homes, parks and gardens.

The current and lifetime chairman is Eileen Kinross, the daughter of one of the founders. The firm's many loyal customers who regularly travel with Seamarks are proof of the company's commitment to offering the best possible value and ensuring that an excursion with Seamarks is a pleasure from beginning to end.

Top: *Staff from Ogden & Cleavers on a day trip to Margate in June 1953.* ***Below:*** *A view of the company's premises as built in 1949.*

Doing very well by making its customers better

When chemist George Wallis first set up in business in Watford with accountant W T J Deverell in 1925, they thought the future of their enterprise lay in analytical chemistry. But within five years they had moved away from this branch of chemistry to concentrate on making tablets for the pharmaceutical industries. The biggest of their early contracts was the manufacture of the original Yeast-Vite, which was marketed to the chemist trade; and from then on this became the focus of their business activities.

Over the next decade the range of tablets manufactured by Wallis had increased greatly, and the company's pioneering work in Unit Packaging brought a growing demand for their competitively-priced, smartly-packed tablets and capsules. In 1958 the company moved into modern factory premises with a large, well-equipped laboratory on Holywell Industrial Estate, Watford. The management of Wallis had by this time passed to W T Deverell, the son of

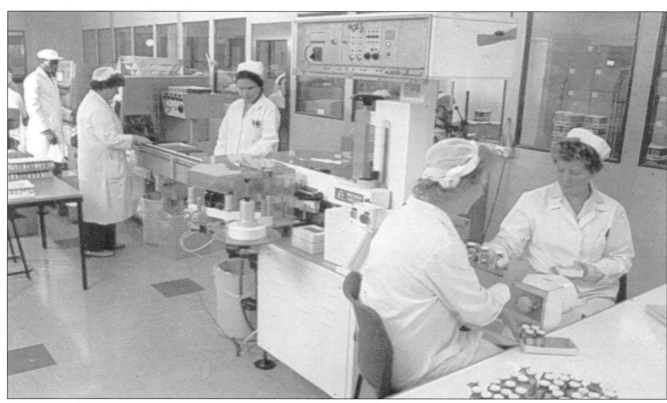

founder W T J Deverell. Expansion continued during the 50s when the company was engaged, under contract to United Africa Company, a subsidiary of UniLever, in the manufacturing and packaging of an Aspirin and Caffeine tablet for the West African markets.

The company's next major breakthrough came during the 1960s when it began manufacturing generic Paracetamol tablets. This proved an instant success, and legislation in the form of the 1968 Medicines Act effectively pruned the pharmaceutical manufacturing industry by introducing more stringent controls which removed the smaller and less well-equipped producers. Subsequently a number of the larger manufacturing companies adopted a policy of concentrating on the major brands to the exclusion of some of their generic products, and this provided opportunities for product development which Wallis

Above: Company product list dating from the early 1960s. Below: Production in the 1980s.

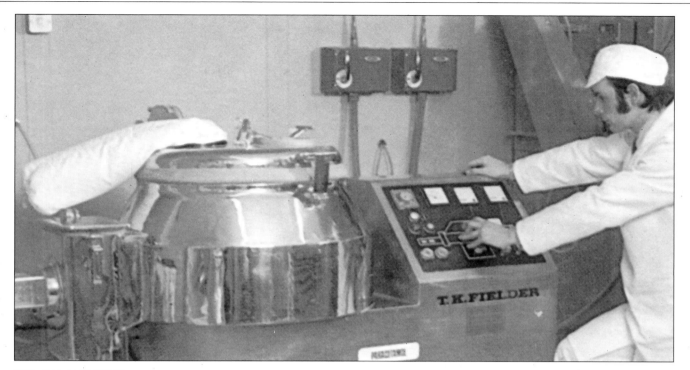

was quick to take up. As the company continued to expand, W T Deverell invited his son P R T Deverell - who, true to the family tradition, had embarked upon a career in accountancy - to join the business.

The 1980s and 90s have seen a number of changes in the management and structure of Wallis. In 1982 the thriving company was acquired by Laporte Industries, the UK's second-largest independent speciality chemicals group. As a result the firm was able to retain its autonomy while benefiting from significant investment in product development and sophisticated manufacturing equipment. In 1994 Wallis returned to the private sector, and in February 1997 it was bought by Wockhardt Limited, a major Indian pharmaceutical manufacturing company which specialises in the production of bulk pharmaceutical raw materials and a wide range of prescription medicines. As part of the Wockhardt group, Wallis is backed by first-class research and development facilities and resources.

Wallis has a wealth of experience in the production of private label medicines for a client list which includes some of the largest UK-based pharmaceutical wholesalers as well as a number of major High Street retailers. Its products are on sale both at pharmacies and in grocery outlets, and are offered for over-the-counter sale under the Pharmacy Only and General Sales List, as the two legal categories are known. The company brings us items as varied as Analgesic

tablets and capsules, Cold Relief products, Artificial Sweeteners and Denture Cleaning Tablets. When 'private label' pharmaceutical items began to appear on the shelves they were initially seen as 'cheap and cheerful' alternatives to big-name brands, but consumer confidence in them has grown. In recent years we have come to recognise that the 'private label' product ranges are high quality, good value alternatives to the major established brands.

At its purpose-built manufacturing plant at Laporte Way, Luton, Wallis Laboratory manufactures billions of tablets, capsules and sachets and many tonnes of granules each year, with a significant proportion destined for the export market. Attractively-packaged traditional tablet, capsule and sachet products account for a high proportion of its output. Throughout its history, the company has combined a keen sensitivity to consumer needs and trends with an innovative approach to products and packaging. The introduction of strip packing was one of Wallis's most successful innovations; the company was also one of the first to replace glass bottles with plastic ones, and was instrumental in introducing child-resistant and tamper-proof packaging ahead of legislation. Maintaining its position at the forefront of developments in packaging, the company is currently looking forward to the commissioning of its new fully-integrated Blister Packaging line which will have the latest code and detection facilities in-built to produce tamper evident bundles.

Other plans for the future include creating new products in-house with the aim of offering an enhanced range, and also adding to the list of 'private label' items through co-operation with other product licence holders with complementary production facilities.

Top: *Working on the machinery during the 1980s.*
Above left: *Paul R.T. Deverell, Managing Director 1976 - 1990.*

The happiest days of their lives

Recent years have seen an increasing trend in education towards regular testing of children's abilities, with the results given great prominence in both local and national press. People living in the Luton area will by now be accustomed to reading of the excellent results achieved by the young pupils at Moorlands School, where year after year targets are regularly met or exceeded by 100 percent of candidates. Children from a wide cross-section of Luton's community come to Moorlands between the ages of two and eleven to learn to work and play together in a happy, friendly and stimulating atmosphere. Classes are small, teaching is traditionally-based, facilities are good, after-school activities cater for the widest possible range of interests and are well-patronised. In these ways the school carefully encourages each child to reach his or her full potential. Exams need hold no terrors for these young people!

Although Moorlands School was founded more than a hundred years ago, in 1891, it only became fully co-educational in the second half of the 20th century; boys had been admitted to the pre-prep school since the 1930s, but the prep school remained open to girls only until 1953. At that time the school was around a quarter of its current size; when it moved to its current location at Leagrave Hall in 1958, there were approximately 80 pupils on the roll. The history of Leagrave Hall has

Above right: Leagrave Hall in the late 19th century.
Below: Official school photograph - 1950.

been thoroughly investigated by the pupils of Moorlands, who can tell us all about the fine mansion which was built by the Filmer family in 1850, sold to wealthy dyer Thomas Lye in 1899, and changed hands another six times before becoming the site of Moorlands School in 1958.

Leagrave Hall is the school's fourth home. The school has always been called Moorlands, and its original site is thought to have been in New Bedford Road, overlooking the Moor. In the 1920s the school moved to Moorlands House in King Street, and the following decade it moved again, to Dunstable Road. A school prospectus from the Dunstable Road period, when Miss Spencer was Principal and Miss Tyson Vice-Principal, informs parents that 'The School course consists of the

usual subjects, which include:- Scripture, English, French, Latin, Mathematics, History, Geography, Nature Study, Elocution Class, Singing, Needlework, and Educational Handwork (including Drawing, Painting, Modelling and Weaving)'; fees for pupils aged between seven and ten were £5.5s.0d per term, with an additional 10/6 (53 pence in today's currency) for stationery and books; optional subjects were on offer, such as Dancing or Pianoforte, each costing £1.11s.6d per term; milk cost 7/6 or 9/6 according to the length of term, and dinner cost £3.10s.0d or £3.15s.0d, again according to length of term.

Although the names given to some of the subjects - not to mention the tuition rates! - make rather quaint reading today, if we replace Latin with Computing then the syllabus is surprisingly close to today's course of study, which is to a large extent based on the Common Entrance syllabus covered in most preparatory schools, and the National Curriculum. In the Pre-prep school, children between the ages of two and three are introduced to pre-literacy, numeracy and writing skills in the Nursery, and in Kindergarten their language, numeracy and reasoning skills are developed. At the age of five they enter the main school; in Lower School they take most of their lessons with their class teacher, and from the age of seven upwards they receive more specialist teaching to

broaden their interests. Since moving to Leagrave Hall, the school has been able to expand. The first addition was the new school hall, which was opened in 1960, and this was followed by a lower school classroom block, built in 1968.

More recent additions include the new gymnasium in 1984, the Science Laboratory in 1996, and the Third Form classroom building in 1998. Moorlands Lodge, a detached property with its own garden and playground, was opened as the school's Nursery in 1997. At the time of writing a Language Laboratory is under construction and is due to open in the summer of 1999.

Throughout the school - Nursery, Kindergarten, Lower and Upper School - every child is treated as an individual; high standards of behaviour, good manners and respect for others are fostered and a family atmosphere is maintained. Moorlands enjoys a reputation for being a happy and friendly school, as well as for achieving excellent academic results - and proud parents throughout Luton, Dunstable and the surrounding villages will agree that both these reputations are well-deserved.

Above: *The official opening of Leagrave Hall by Sir John Burgoyne, October 1960.* ***Top:*** *School sports, Wardown Park in 1959.* ***Left:*** *The current Headmaster, A J Cook.*

Fresh Milk and Eggs on your doorstep

Tom Sheaf, founder of the independent Sheaf's Dairy, went to work, in the 1920s when in his early teens, for his grandfather, Mr Bonnick, who owned Winsdon Dairies in Russell Street. In those days dairies actually produced their own milk from their own cows in the fields which, in this case, are now Meyrick Avenue and Bonnick Close. The dairy men were totally responsible for the clean state of milk before pasteurisation became common. Anyone who has hand milked well behaved, let alone awkward, cows in the fields, or in straw and dung strewn byres, will know how easy it was for dirt to enter the open buckets then in use.

Once the milk had been taken from the, generally placid, beasts with traditional names like Daisy, Buttercup and Florence it was carried to the dairy where it was tipped into the tub above the cooler. From this it ran, in the open air, down a corrugated water cooled cooler rather like granny's old wash day scrubber before passing through a paper filter into the churn. This 12 or 17 gallon, multiply by four for litres, steel container was manhandled over to the adjacent bottling machine into which the milk was poured, again in the open air of the well scrubbed dairy.

This simple machine could be altered to fill one third pint bottles for school children, half pint, pint or the fat quart (2 pint) bottles for families, in those unrefrigerated days customers needed such choice as milk did not keep long. The bottles, printed with the dairy's name, were hand capped with labelled cardboard circles, the centre of which could be poked out so that the top could be lifted from the bottle.

Above left: *Tom Sheaf, founder of Sheafs Dairies.*
Below: *Delivering milk in the 1920s.*

Apart from the widespread introduction of milking machines by the late 1940s this was the normal procedure for bottling milk until the 1950s.

Tom Sheaf and his wife Rena started their own dairy at 214 Wellington Street in 1936. They bought some fifty gallons a day from local farmers, which she bottled for him to deliver. During the war Tom was in the Royal Artillary driving lorries carrying 'Ack Ack' guns up and down the Norfolk Coast. When not on duty with the Royal Artillary he was in the Home Guard and Rena carried on the milk round single handed, taking their baby, their fourth child, on the round tucked up in a washing basket.

By 1954 they had outgrown their original premises and moved from one side of Wellington Street to the other and decided that pasteurised milk, rapidly heated and cooled to kill microbes, was the milk of the future. To survive in a changing world they extended the range of goods carried by shop and floats to include eggs and cream, bread and potatoes. As tastes changed they stocked yoghurt, bottled mineral waters and flavoured milks and today carry tea bags, cooking foil, bin liners and garden products. By the late 1970s they were delivering 1500 gallons of milk daily, and made a move to purpose built premises on Latimer Road.

As a result of the family's ability to assess the needs of their customers who include offices and factories, Sheaf's Dairy is a highly regarded part of the Luton scene. In spite of the difficulties of competing with local factories and offices for staff to start work in the 'wee ghastlies' of the dawn before it's properly lit the family firm offers a real service to its doorstep customers. A milkman who thinks of popping your bottles in the shade, or of calling to see that elderly customers are bright eyed and bushy tailed, is a treasure, not least when his stock saves your bacon after the kids polished off the last of the bread earmarked for tea.

Under the direction of David, Michael and Peter, three of the founder's seven children, the go ahead company buys in bottled milk for delivery by a fleet of smart nippy milk floats. The roundsmen arrive at around 4am to start their shift for loading and are off on the rounds to reach as many homes in time for breakfast as is possible. Milkmen and women are cheerful, fit outdoor types who enjoy responsibility and the customer contact which is a vital part of a public service unique to Britain.

Top: *The interior of Latimer Road premises in the late 1970s.* ***Above Left:*** *Tom Sheaf celabrating with a glass of milk at the official opening of the Latimer Road premises.*

Supplying the things that matter to the hatter

Hats, as everybody in Luton knows, are an essential part of life; and braids and hoods are an essential part of hats. For 45 years Luton hat manufacturers have been relying on the Fischer family to provide them with the things they need, and today they can count on the same high quality of service and of product, the same personal attention and the same quick efficient delivery as when the company began.

Mr Willy Fischer began trading in Luton as an import and export merchant in May 1934, acting as an agent for a Swiss braid manufacturer and supplying the hat trade with braids and hoods to make into ladies hats.

On 23rd June 1954 the new company was formed - W Fischer & Sons (Luton) Ltd. which included Willy Fischer's two sons, Peter and Eric, who have now been joined by Alan, representing the third generation.

The business has diversified a little over the years in order to adapt to changes in the trading pattern. There has been a trend for large stores to force their smaller competitors out of business, and this, combined with the increased number of cash and carry warehouses which now play a significant role in distribution, has resulted in W Fischer & Sons Limited carrying a wider range of stock and dealing with a greater variety of customers. The company began by dealing in synthetic braids, Chinese natural hoods, wool hoods and imitation fur material. Chinese natural hoods have remained an important stock item, but Fischer can also supply swimwear, children's clothing and parasols, as well as children's hats, ladies' hats, men's hats - and of course the ubiquitous baseball cap! Items such as these are supplied in quantity to cash and carry warehouses from Glasgow to Bristol, who along with the Luton hat manufacturers form Fischer & Sons Limited's clientele.

With customers in all the major British cities - Birmingham, Manchester, Liverpool, Leeds and Newcastle - Fischer also exports goods to Ireland and Holland. The company has accumulated a vast amount of experience of this specialised trade over the years, and this, combined with its philosophy of always treating the customer fairly, makes it a company which clients enjoy dealing with. It is refreshing, these days, to find a successful, well-respected family business with satisfied customers which is also satisfied with its own success, and is not tempted to sacrifice its traditional values in the pursuit of ever-increasing profits.

Below: *From left to right: Eric Fischer, Willy Fischer, Thomas Gill, Mr Bruggisser (a Swiss supplier) and Peter Fischer.*

From fireman to hotelier

Monty Rosen is a former fireman who then became a builder before starting his real career move to become a well known local hotelier. During his building years he collected ideas from the houses and sites where he worked. These were stored away until, in 1970, the opportunity arose to buy two adjacent "semi's" already converted to 'bedsits'. Monty saw the potential of the distinctive inter-war house and its attached neighbour both with sizeable gardens for future expansion. He bought the existing business, which had just five letting rooms, and decided on a full scale expansion rather than piecemeal work around the guests.

The work of extension and upgrading was started and finished in 1976. Like so many people who wish to alter their homes into business premises he found the planners as cautious a breed as bankers. Fortunately his two sons, J P and S A, both chartered surveyors, were able to make light work of protective legislation by producing very acceptable plans for change of use. Steven and Jeff assisted with the multiple facets of the on site work during reconstruction. Although a lot of the garden areas have been converted to essential car parking for a mobile clientele the landscaped front offers a green welcome to guests.

For sound advertising reasons the hotel was named The Arlington as the letter A is found in the first pages of the telephone book. AA registration and commendations attract those who like to be sure of high standards while at the same time avoiding the standardised offerings of chain hotels.

Monty and Francis Rosen, and their skilled staff, Mandy Short, Liz Roberts and Richay Roberts provide friendly caring hospitality to guests in 22 rooms, of which 19 are en-suite for those who value private facilities. Many of their regular visitors are people who stay all week, working away from home for five days and returning for weekend visits, leaving their hotel rooms free for weekend tourists.

Below: *The Hotel's Dining Room.*

This picture: *The Arlington Hotel.*

The family with a head for business and a hat for every occasion

Different countries may have different fashions, but a good craftsman is a good craftsman the world over; so when Mr A L Heymann came over from Germany to live in Luton, the skills he had learned whilst working in a relative's hat factory in Dresden stood him in good stead. He got a job with A & C Simpson, and stayed with the company for seven years; then in June 1946 Lutz, as he had become known, decided it was time to start his own business.

With a workforce of eight, in back rooms in Crawley Road, Luton, the little hat firm began manufacture. They followed the traditional methods, using wood blocks to produce felt and straw hats. Lutz himself took a hand in production, and as well as obtaining materials - which in the early years was not always easy, as many items were in short supply - he also handled sales. Customers liked the factory's hand-made, high quality products, and within five years the firm had moved to better premises in Clarendon Road.

Over the years the family firm has built up an invaluable store of experience and expertise in the millinery industry, as well as an excellent understanding of their customers' requirements, and hats made by Marida can be found at speciality shops and stores both in this country and abroad.

For more than half a century Marida has helped Luton maintain its traditional reputation as the centre of hat manufacturing, ensuring that the skills of the trade are kept alive and providing continuous employment for craft workers. The firm has taken advantage of developments in the industry, and gas pans are now used instead of wood blocks, while employees enjoy all the comforts of a modern working environment at Dudley Street, which has been Marida's home since March 1960.

Today Marida is run by Lutz's daughter Marian and continues to use traditional methods to manufacture felt and straw hats of the very highest quality, together with a selection of fabric hats. Customers of all ages will find hats to tempt them amongst Marida's range, whether they are looking for something casual, or something smart, or a hat for a special occasion - or just browsing!

Above: *Princess Anne's visit to Marida in 1988.*
Below: *The sewing room as it used to look.*

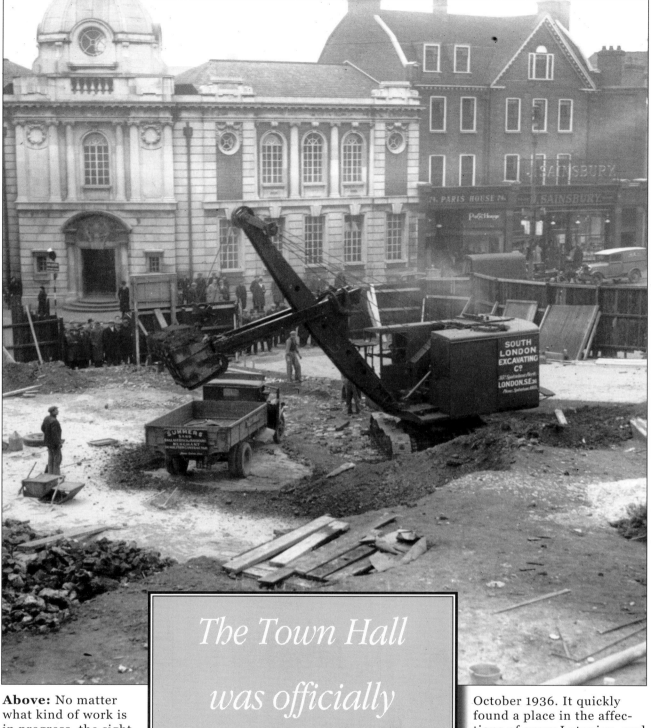

The Town Hall was officially opened on 28th October 1936

Above: No matter what kind of work is in progress, the sight of men working has always attracted passers-by to watch them; dig a hole anywhere, and a crowd of people will gather to gaze into it! The building work that had attracted this particular crowd was the building of the new Town Hall in 1935. Work on the splendid new building went on apace, and the Duke of Kent declared the Town Hall officially open on 28th October 1936. It quickly found a place in the affections of every Lutonian, and is today the town's most well-known landmark. The elegant building in the background is the Carnegie Library - Andrew Carnegie's generous donation to the town - opened in October 1910. Even though the fine new library with its wide range of facilities was much appreciated, the demolition of the Carnegie Library in the early 1960s was condemned by many Lutonians who were sad to see the beautiful building go.

It was 1st September 1939, and though war had not yet been officially declared, the evacuation of children who lived in high-risk areas was a priority.

Acknowledgments

The Luton News and Mr John Buckledee (editor); Mr and Mrs E.G. Meadows; Luton Central Library; Mr Nigel Lutt and Bedfordshire and Luton Archives and Record Service; Mrs Jackie White and Luton W.R.V.S; Mr Eamonn Hart.

Thanks are also due to
Peggy Burns who penned the editorial text
Mark Stubbs of Luton Central Library, editorial consultant
Margaret Wakefield and Mike Kirke for their copywriting skills